DUMB THINGS I'M GLAD I DID

I0555371

MICHAEL J. ENGSTROM

GEMLIGHT
PUBLISHING LLC

Fort Worth ,Texas

Copyright © 2023 by Michael J. Engstrom

ISBN: 979-8-218-25365-3

Printed in the United States of America

Publisher: Gemlight Publishing LLC

9500 Ray White Rd, Ste 200

Fort Worth. Texas 76244

817-745-4556

www.gemlightpublishiing.com

Preface:

My middle school years were the most difficult years of my life, although that's not saying much. I went to elementary school in Cottage Grove, MN and had great friends — the best being Dan Weston and Tom Lord. We spent summer days playing hot box, riding bikes all over town, and going to Super America for Laffy Taffy and Big-League Chew while working up the courage to talk to girls.

Life was simple, but life was great. It was exactly the way it should be for an eleven-year-old boy. That summer, my dad had a job opportunity in Fort Worth, TX and the family moved just like that.

Seventh grade was difficult. I don't remember much of it, but I know that without my newfound friends, Steve and David, it would have been unbearable. I was in a strange school and tensions at home were high with my older brother getting into serious trouble and hanging out with the wrong crowd.

I spent most of my time playing basketball in the backyard by myself, and I could tell that things weren't quite right between my parents. By the end of that year, we had decided that my mom, my brother, and I would move back to Minnesota. We found an apartment back in Cottage Grove right before the school year began.

Eighth grade was a much bigger challenge than I had predicted. So much of the social construct in eighth grade was decided the prior year. Only one-third of the Oaltman Jr. High student body came from my elementary school. An entire year had passed in which the social hierarchy was established, and I was left out.

I played football and although better than most, that doesn't carry much weight in a state where putting a puck in the net is exponentially more important than scoring a touchdown or picking off a pass.

My mom was miserable. We were living in low-income apartments, and she was working long hours and was no doubt dealing with my brother's indiscretions. I didn't realize it at the time, but she sacrificed so much that year and I'm forever grateful. By the end of that year, we were on our way back to Texas where my dad had purchased a home in the suburban community of Mansfield.

Although I thought it was the end of the world at the time, it was part of God's plan for my life. Texas was where I met the friends who make up the stories in this book. It was where I met my wife, made my career, and raised my kids. Even though I have fond memories of Minnesota and occasionally keep in touch with Tom and Dan, Texas was home and likely always will be.

Now, more than thirty years later, my life is probably like that of many middle-aged men. Most of my time is spent at work and with my family. Although life is busy, I still find time to hang out with several of the friends that I met in high school. Much of our current interaction centers around our fantasy football league.

Once a year, we'd rent a lake house, suffer through a frustrating draft process where the twins take forever to pick, play dominoes and poker, drink too much on Friday, and hit the lake to wind down the following day. Every year, we joke that it was a good run, and we are too old for it. However, by the following weekend, we are all counting the days to next August to do it all over again.

We often relive some of the wild pranks and best memories from our high school and college days. This book is simply a collection of many of those stories. As you read our stories, you may believe us to be miscreants, but we turned out just fine. In our group, we have a firefighter, a secret service agent, a teacher, a television personality, a college professor, and several successful businessmen. On that weekend however, the collective maturity level is reduced by a few decades per person.

Finally, to quote George Costanza, "These stories have not been embellished, because they need no embellishment." These are simply my stories retold to the best of my memory with a little help from my friends.

[One of our recent draft weekends]

Background

Mansfield, TX in the early 90s was a much different town than it is today. It was a sleepy town with a population of approximately 15,000. There was one high school and a rodeo. We didn't have a movie theater or a shopping mall, so we had to drive to Arlington to enjoy those types of activities. There was one McDonald's so even a Taco Bell run required a road trip.

Our 1992 senior class was around 300 kids, so it was big enough to feel like we were on the map but small enough to know just about everyone.

My guess is that our high school experience was like most who would read this book. The social life centered around high school sporting events, parties, and whatever dumb stuff you could dream up with your friends. To start, I'll provide a little background on the main characters who frequently appear throughout these stories.

Dave Jimenez

Dave was one of my first friends I met on the football team when I moved to Mansfield in 9th grade, and he remains my best friend to this day. We served as best man at each other's weddings and still see each other several times a year. He met his wife, Kelly, at Stephen F. Austin University (SFA), and they have two boys, Landry and Luke. Dave teaches SPED in the Mansfield School District.

Ian Martin (Ebone)

Ian was the center of our high school basketball team, and you could never miss his big frame coming down the hallways. He went to Texas A&M, dropped out, joined the army, did time overseas, and eventually came back to graduate before becoming a Dallas firefighter. We stayed in touch through all of that and still see each other several times a year. He lives with his wife, Trish, and daughter, Emmy, in Garland, TX.

Joe Thomas

Joe's house was home base for much of high school. His parents were awesome and never minded us meeting there to play pool and come up with a plan for the night. Joe went to LSU, and we kept in touch. We visited him in Baton Rouge, and he made a couple of visits to SFA. He received his graduate degree from SMU. We still hang out several times a year. He lives in Grapevine, TX with his wife, Alexis, and their son, Grayson.

Kelly Duren

Kelly was the point guard of the basketball team, prom king, and whatever other popularity awards you can give out. He moved to a few different colleges before graduating from Southwest TX State. Kelly and I remained friends throughout high school and college. We ended up living together for three to four years after college until I got married. We stayed close friends into our 30s but eventually fell out of touch. We spoke a few times recently when we attended Omar's father's funeral and when I asked him for permission to share these old stories. He lives in Athens, TX with his wife. I'll do a better job of reaching out more often.

Mike Jones

Mike was our class president. Although he was one of the most popular kids in school, he wasn't even the most popular member of his family. His dad, Danny, was a long-time art teacher at Mansfield High and approached his profession with such passion and grace that he ended up with a school named after him. Mike graduated from Southwest TX State. We stayed in contact throughout college and into our late twenties, but we eventually lost touch. I recently caught up with him over this book, and it was fun reliving some old memories together. He lives in Wimberly, TX with his wife. His parents, Danny and Lynn, also live in Wimberly, TX and I hope to see them again someday soon.

David Vaillancourt

David was on the basketball team in high school and went on to play junior college ball before transferring to Texas A&M. He then got his masters and doctorate from Penn State. He is a research and teaching professor at the University of Florida where he lives with his wife, Laura, and their three daughters. We never lost touch and see each other every year at draft weekend as well as the occasional visits when schedules allow.

Fred Brandenburg

Fred was on the football team, and we have stayed in frequent contact over the past thirty years. Fred is an investment professional living in Castle Rock, CO with his wife, Dawn. They have three daughters, and Fred is the first official grandpa of our league as his oldest is a Mizzu grad and living back in the area after getting married. Fred went to SFA and preceded me in the KA fraternity which is one of the reasons I joined. We usually see each other on draft weekend and maybe one other time per year if vacation or business travel allows.

Fred and his brother, Mark, were the comedy twins in our class and are still two of the funniest people I have met. I still remember when Fred and I were standing in the hall after lunch and a freshman came up to ask if we would donate to their choir trip. Without hesitation, Fred began to sing in a high octave, "Noooooooo!"

Mark Brandenburg

Mark and Fred are twins. After high school, Mark played football at a small catholic school in KS and then became a police officer before joining the secret service. He published a novel, *Fence Jumper*, earlier this year. Mark lives in the DC area with his wife, and they have a son at Virginia Tech. Mark is a constant fixture at our fantasy football weekend and is a consistent source of comedy in our group chat.

Cade Hudson

Cade was the center and captain of our high school football team, and he served our country as an Army Ranger. We lost touch with Cade over the years, but we reconnected while I was writing this book. He got remarried to an old high school flame and is living in Burleson, TX.

Jason Verhagen

Jason and I were friends in high school but got to know each other better in college and even better as adults. I see him every year at draft and usually at least a few other times throughout the year. When he was 46, we renamed him, and he shall henceforth be known as "PCHOP." He lives in Frisco, TX with his wife, Ashley, whom he met at SFA. They have four kids.

Danny Price

Danny and I met on the football team and were friends in high school. Much like Jason, we became better friends throughout the years and into adulthood. We see each other every draft and several other times throughout the year. Danny met his wife, Michelle, at SFA. They live in Prosper, TX and have three daughters. Danny is a world traveler and seems to vacation in Mexico about once a month.

Omar Trevino

One of the things that surprised me when I started jotting these stories down is that Omar isn't more prominently featured. Trouble followed Omar, or more accurately put, Omar followed trouble. He was with us most weekends but somehow missed many of the adventures in this book likely due to his soccer or job schedule. He went to LSU and moved back to the DFW area after graduation. We hung out quite a bit in our twenties, but we fell out of touch after we each got married. I recently saw him at his father's funeral where he did an amazing job with the eulogy. He lives in Dallas with his wife, Amanda, and their son and daughter.

Tony Liebelt

Tony played on the basketball team and went on to play junior college ball. He later transferred to Texas A&M where he graduated. Tony started dating one of our classmates our senior year, and they have been together ever since. They have four boys and live somewhere in the DFW area. Tony and I lost touch after high school.

Mike Engstrom (Inky)

I moved to Mansfield in 1988 and played football which is where I met many of the guys. I received my bachelors from SFA and an MBA from UT Arlington. I live in Keller, TX with my wife, Addie, our son, Josh, and our daughter, Maya.

CHAPTER

I n the 90s, the Methodist Church off Walnut Creek Drive in Mansfield would have open gym nights on Sunday evenings where several buddies and I would go play pickup basketball.

It was the summer of 1992. Mike, Tony, Joe, Dave, and I were hanging out after one of these pickup sessions wondering what we should do for the rest of the night. There were no social activities on the calendar, and we were all in the mood for some level of adventure.

After several minutes of discussion in the parking lot, the conversation centered around one topic. There was a new feature in town in the form of a large inflatable Ronald McDonald who spent most of his hours perched high atop the McDonald's at Hwy 287 and Walnut Creek Drive. The more we talked, the more we became certain that son of a bitch had to come down. We agreed to shower and meet in an hour to come up with the game plan.

Any crew worth their salt needed a base to plan such a herculean task. By the time we had all showered, it was past 10:00 and given it was a Sunday night, we couldn't very well have an entire team over to any of our houses with our parents working the next morning. By the time I graduated high school, I didn't have much of a curfew and my parents went to bed early so it was easy to slip in and out at odd times. Apparently, my friends had similar setups with their folks because we soon found ourselves at the Brandenburg's place, ready to nail down the details for our heist.

Fred and Mark Brandenburg were twin brothers and good friends of ours. They were away on vacation with their parents somewhere on a beach, but we knew that they left the garage door open just enough to let the cats come and go. Being 5'8" and 140 lbs. had its disadvantages on the football field, but it sure came in handy when you needed to shimmy under a 10" opening. I was able to get into the garage and then into the house. Within seconds, I had unlocked the front door for the rest of the crew. We now had a comfortable base with no distractions, so we began to plot.

The detailed plan consisted of driving to McDonald's, taking Ronald, bringing him back to the Brandenburg's, and then deciding the next course of action. Dave's parents had splurged and gotten him a used Jeep Wrangler before our senior year. It was a generous gift, not only for their son, but for all of us because we enjoyed countless hours of cruising with the top and doors off, off-roading, and pushing the limits of what teenage drivers should do. Outside of our criminal intellect, the Jeep was our most valuable asset that night.

Our one mistake was that we took only one vehicle, the Jeep, to scout out the scene. As we pulled into McDonald's to assess the situation, it was well past midnight and Walnut Creek Dr. had only the occasional passer-by so we decided to launch right into the action.

In 1992, McDonald's was the only establishment at the NW corner of Walnut Creek and 287. There was a Pizza Inn a couple of hundred yards west down Walnut Creek with an empty lot full of brush and trees in between. We decided that Tony, Dave, and I would scale the ladder to get a closer look at the situation. Mike would hide behind the dumpster to keep watch while Joe would exit the parking lot in the Jeep and wait behind Pizza Inn with the lights off.

As we used the ladder affixed to the building, we were comforted to find that once on the roof, there was a 3-foot exterior wall that you could easily duck behind to remain invisible to any on-coming traffic. It was also comforting to learn that the deflated Ronald McDonald lying limp on the roof was already attached to the blower, so there was only one piece we would need to take to complete the first phase of our mission.

We had been on the roof for less than three minutes studying the connective straps when we heard Mike yell, "cops" and a marked police car entered the parking lot. We were certain that they had either seen us climbing up the ladder or a concerned citizen had seen what we were up to and called the cops. We ducked behind the protective barrier, whispering about what story we wanted to tell the police that would garner the least possible blowback.

To our surprise, the officers never got out of the car. After a minute, they exited the parking lot and proceeded to go east over the bridge and out of sight. The near encounter had spooked Tony, who was ready to abort, but we knew this was our chance to pull off one of the greatest pranks in Mansfield history.

Within seconds, Joe came back into the parking lot, turned the lights off, and parked in the drive-through right next to the ladder. We unplugged Ronald, cut the fasteners with the hedge clippers we took from the Brandenburg's garage, and started feeding him down to Mike and Joe. They began stuffing him in the back seat of the Jeep. Even deflated, he was so large that we couldn't keep him from spilling out over the roll bars. We realized that Ronald took up the entire back seat, so Dave and I proceeded to run Ronald back to base camp while the others waited in the bank parking lot across the street for Dave to return to pick them up.

Even though the Brandenburg's house was only five minutes from McDonald's, this was the riskiest part of the mission. Dave and I knew that if we were pulled over for any reason, we would not be able to explain away our cargo. We also knew that the officer we had seen minutes earlier was somewhere in the area.

We made it safely back to the Brandenburg's house. After we unloaded the cargo, Dave went back to pick up the guys. We sprawled the massive, deflated balloon on the living room floor, took a couple of pictures, and then went back to work on the next phase of the mission. We weighed several options, including: leaving him in the house for the Brandenburg's to find when they returned home, blowing him up in our friend David Vaillancourt's backyard and letting him float in their pool, or show our admiration for one of our more attractive female classmates by inflating him in one of their front yards.

We finally settled on a plan of action: The Mansfield Country Club. It was a short drive from the Brandenburg's and didn't create a specific connection to any of us. By now, we knew we needed two vehicles to transport ourselves and the clown. We decided that since we were already in for a penny, we might as well be in for a pound, so we took Mark's keys and used the Brandenburg's Mustang as our second vehicle. We made our way to the tennis court area at the country club where there were outlets between each set of courts. It could not have been easier. I thought it would take hours to blow up this behemoth, but as soon as we plugged him in, his leg began to grow at such a rapid rate that it sent us scrambling for our vehicles. Seconds later, as we turned on Country Club Dr., we could see Ronald's fully inflated head start to emerge and peek over the tennis courts at us.

After letting the adrenalin wear down, we mustered up the courage to head back and take a few pics with the ginormous clown. Joe T, not pictured, was our cameraman. This was before the days of camera phones when pictures had to be developed. He took the film to the next county to avoid recognition. Although we all thought that was an unnecessary move fueled by paranoia, I have to say now that it was a stroke of genius.

By this time in the story, it was almost daybreak and we knew McDonald's opened at 6:00 am for breakfast. We were unable to suppress the urge to pull through the drive-through for some egg McMuffins and casually ask the attendant, "What happened to the inflatable Ronald?"

Rumors flew around for a few weeks and even though too many knew who was behind the heist, we never had to answer for it. Ronald was eventually returned safely to his home with no damage. No harm, no foul.

My last comment is probably my favorite part of this story. The Brandenburg's were certainly in our inner circle and were some of the first to be let in on the prank when they returned from vacation. As we recounted that evening's events and were showing the guys the recently developed photos, we came across the pictures of home base and the deflated Ronald taking up their entire living room. The look of admiration and awe on Mark's face quickly turned to one of confusion. By the second picture, he was asking "Wait, where the !*#@ were you guys?"

[Left to right: Me, Mike, Tony, Dave.
Joe was the photographer.]

CHAPTER

DOUBLE HEADER

It was late summer after high school graduation when Cade, Ian, Dave, Mark, Fred, Kelly and I were all together with no discernable direction for the night. Ian just got his buzz cut as he was preparing to leave for A&M where he would join the Corps. The rest of us could feel the end of the summer approaching at a rapid speed.

We had done all of the usual things which consisted of going by the 7-11 several times as well as the old, abandoned Arbors development to see if any of our female classmates were out driving around or if an unplanned party sprang up.

With no luck, we turned our attention to something a bit more dangerous. The Texas Rangers were on a road trip, and since we were only 30 minutes from the ballpark, we began to scheme a way to get into the stadium. For those familiar with the old Rangers ballparks, Arlington Stadium is the one that preceded The Ballpark in Arlington which was built in 1995 and preceded the current venue. It was a glorified minor league field, but it was home to our beloved Rangers like Ruben Sierra and Julio Franco. Therefore, it was held in high regard. Per our normal modus operandi, we just started driving and figured we'd have a plan by the time we arrived. Dave and I worked parking for the Rangers our junior year and leveraged every bit of our inside intel. What that meant was we simply got out of the car, took down the chain, and drove into the parking lot.

I wish I could say we came up with a clever plan to get inside, but the reality was by the time we began brainstorming, Cade had scaled the fence and was belittling us for not keeping up. A few seconds later, we all jumped the fence and were walking through one of the first base sections down to the field. We didn't really have a game plan, so we rounded the bases, slid into second, sat in the dugout, checked out the mound, and tried unsuccessfully to place calls between the dugout and bullpen.

Barely 20 minutes later, we had run out of things to do but the night was early and we were riding high with confidence after another successful mission. The conversation was predictable. If we can get into the ballpark that easily, why not up the ante? Major league baseball was one thing, but in Texas, it began and ended with the Cowboys. Back then, the Cowboys played at Texas Stadium in Irving which was another 30 minutes or so from the first base dugout we were sitting in. Based on one suggestion and a quick nod from each man, we were on our way out of the ballpark and on our way to Texas Stadium.

We were split into two cars and given there were no cell phones, each car was devising the best plan to get in and out without being nabbed by the 5.0 or Cowboy's security. Since I was not in Cade's car, our planning was irrelevant. We once again found ourselves scaling a fence within seconds of parking. Soon, we were in. A secondary fence needed to be negotiated. That may have been a problem for lesser athletes but not us. We soon found ourselves running down the aisles in the lower sections to take the short jump from the stands to the field.

Ian was behind me, and he took a picture while we were descending the steps. I had no idea where the flash came from, and I thought for sure we had been busted. However, my friends seemed unwavering in their pursuit, so I just kept going.

Once on the field, we didn't have much to do. It was dark and we didn't have a football, so we ran a few mock plays, scored a couple of fantasized touchdowns, and then took a picture on the star at midfield. I apologize for the centerpiece of the photo, but if you can avert your eyes from Ian's behind, you will be able to see that we are right at midfield.

[From left to right: Dave, Cade, me, Ian, Fred. Mark or Kelly must have taken the photo of us sitting in the Ranger's dugout.]

[Fred and I on the left with Ian's ass right behind us. Cade in the background, Kelly in the hat, and Dave was lying on the star at midfield. Mark took the picture.]

[All of us under the Cowboy's goalpost.]

[Fred, Mark, Dave, Cade, Ian, and I reveling in the night's success after we got back. I assume Kelly was taking the picture.]

CHAPTER

TRADING PUNCHES

There was one random weekend during our senior year where Mike Jones had the house to himself since his parents and younger sister were out of town. Mike was a bit more of a rule follower than the rest of us, but he had decided to throw a small get together at his house. Pretty much all the guys in the other stories were there along with some others and several of the girls in our graduating class.

I still can't recall exactly what prompted the idea but somehow, Kelly and I got into a serious conversation about trading punches. Whether it was true or not, we both considered ourselves tougher than most. We had been in enough scrapes to feel confident that we could receive and deliver a punch. The discussion started with about five of us, but the others were thinking more clearly and declined to participate in the shenanigans.

After a while, we found ourselves down at the end of Mike's street ready to trade blows. A couple of the guys came out to witness the act of idiocy but most could not be torn away from the party or simply believed nothing would happen. Kelly and I were buddies, so we were moving forward strictly in the scientific sense of seeing how hard we could punch someone. There wasn't any animosity between us which made it easier to set the ground rules. As we advanced toward the moment of truth, we decided we would stand still and face to the side. This would make our full profile available and would provide an adequate target. We would avoid broken noses or mouth injuries by focusing squarely on the jaw.

It was my turn to punch first. He stood facing sideways and just as promised, he did not flinch. My punch was true and solid. I had never hit anyone that hard before and he fell to the ground immediately after my knuckles connected.

As I was helping him up, I remember asking, "Are you mad?" I thought for a minute this might not turn out well.

He was a true gentleman and said, "no." He said he just needed a minute to "gather himself."

It was Kelly's turn. I also kept my word and remained perfectly still as his right hook came down toward my face. The punch landed with great force, and I also hit the deck. As he helped me up and let me collect myself, we did the bro hug and shared a quick laugh before heading back to Mike's house.

I still remember what I was wearing. The previous summer, I had worked parking for the Texas Rangers and one of my prized possessions was a white T-shirt with the words "Oakland Sucks" spelled out in their green and gold color combo. As we entered the house to claim whatever odd victory came from punching each other, the house stopped, and all eyes turned toward us. A few of the girls came running up to ask if I was okay.

We hadn't realized it, but Kelly's blow had caught enough of my lip that it pierced my eye tooth. In the short time it took to walk back to Mike's house, the blood had began to soak my favorite shirt and I was a hot mess by the time we entered the front door. We downplayed it and reveled in whatever imagined glory came from such a ridiculous stunt.

It was late, and the party began to clear out. I remember taking Joe into the bathroom to look in the mirror and asking him to level with me about my lip. He said he was pretty sure we needed to get to a hospital for stitches, so we consulted Mike to help take a closer look. He agreed that the lip was punctured all the way through, and we did need to make a road trip.

Mike drove me up to the Arlington hospital where we received two pieces of news. First, the doctor confirmed that there was a hole in my lip and if I didn't get stitches, and soon, there would be some permanent damage. Second, since I was 17 at the time, I needed a parent to either accompany me or call the hospital and give them permission to perform the procedure.

Next stop: my house to wake up my dad and explain the situation.

My version was a complete lie. I told my dad we had been playing basketball at Mike's, and I had taken an elbow to the mouth.

He simply said, "Must have been a sharp elbow."

Even though he didn't buy my story, he didn't challenge it. He opted to call the hospital and let Mike run me around. By 4:00 a.m., I had my stitches, and we were back at Mike's house to catch some shut eye.

The next morning, we relived the previous night's events with the other guys over breakfast at McDonald's where some obnoxious inflatable balloon had no idea what we had in store for it.

As I look back on this story, I can't imagine my son coming home in the middle of the night needing stitches and me outsourcing the logistics to one of his friends. You may view that comment as a criticism of my dad...

CHAPTER

DIKE'S DETECTIVE AGENCY

I was riding around with Dave, Kelly, and Ian one random weekend during our senior year. We knew Julie's parents were out of town. She was a friend and one of the more attractive and popular girls in our grade. Even though she wasn't throwing a party, we had stopped by to say hello. When she let us in, she immediately began to complain that her sister, two years younger, was supposed to be home for the night but was nowhere to be found. We formed DIKE's detective agency on the spot and accepted the mission of finding her sister and bringing her home. The name was derived from Dave, Inky, Kelly, and Ebone, but we thought it played on many levels.

Keep in mind that this was before the age of text messages and social media, so the mission was a bit more complicated than it would have been now. I can't remember exactly how we went about it, but I was dating a friend of Julie's sister and we knew her sister had a boyfriend. It didn't take seasoned detectives to figure out the first stop was maybe her boyfriend's house. I cannot recall how we found his address, but it likely involved getting his last name from my girlfriend and referencing the white pages.

As the four of us approached the front door, we decided it was best to let Ian's 6'5" frame stand looming in the background as we assumed a two-by-two position with me and Kelly in the front.

The boyfriend answered the door, and we asked for Paula. He claimed she wasn't there, but anyone could see he was nervous about something. He had his friends over, and they assumed a supportive position behind him in the front foyer. He was going to shut the door until I put my hand out to stop it from closing. I think it was Kelly who calmly said, "Go get her."

There was a brief moment of tension with the crew that was one year our junior, but we were the alpha males of this showdown and refused to back down. Not wanting to tussle, they brought her to the door where we told her Julie needed her back home and she was to come with us. We escorted her in two-by-two formation back to the car. We didn't really know what we were doing, but we had taken the roles to heart and were being as official as possible. We were even keeping the dialogue between the four of us to a level of professionalism that we assumed real detectives would show. She was sandwiched between Dave and I in the backseat and cried most of the way home.

As we entered her home, Julie unleashed a verbal tirade that could have made a sailor blush and her sister ran back through the hall and out of sight. Julie thanked us and asked where she had been. We told her she didn't want to know and then reminded her that we were now an official detective agency and didn't do charity cases. I can't recall what we accepted as payment, but I'm 80% sure it was a box of Cheez-Its and four Dr. Peppers from her pantry.

CHAPTER

WHERE'S MIKE'S TRUCK?

Joe's house was often the meeting spot before we would go out for the night. He had a pool table, a great basketball court in the backyard, and his parents, Ray and Mary, were always open to having the boys over. I can't remember what the particular festivities were for the night, but I know that Craig, Mike, and David V. were in one car and Joe, Dave, Fred, and I were in another. After our night out, we had gotten back to Joe's house and knew that we had about a 20 minute gap before the other guys would arrive.

Mike Jones drove an old Chevy truck, and it was parked in front of Joe's house. It was a manual transmission with three on the tree and was useless to lock because it had a small secondary triangular window that you could just push open, reach in, and unlock the door.

With 20 minutes to kill, the prank seemed obvious. We put the truck in neutral and started pushing it down the street. Originally, we were just going to move it a few houses down Chesnutt street and see if we could get a rise out of Mike. After realizing how easy it was to push and direct, we ended up pushing it down the entire street, took a right, and parked it a block over.

We were waiting in Joe's yard for the guys to return and were delighted when we saw the headlights from David's Jeep Cherokee. After they stepped out, we all began to talk about the video games at the arcade or whatever it was we were up to earlier that evening.

After several minutes and a moment of recognition, Mike threw his hat on the ground and was obviously flustered. He began to explain that he had driven to Joe's earlier that evening and left his truck parked on the street which meant it must have been stolen. Our acting performance was superb as we grilled Mike about his keys and asked if he was sure he drove to Joe's. We also gave other plausible reasons the truck could be missing. The best part was, since Craig and David V. were not in on it, they also played both sides and questioned if Mike had driven to Joe's earlier that night. The best line was when David V. asked Mike, "No offense, but who would want to steal your truck?"

Just before he was about to call his dad or the cops, we somehow convinced him to take a quick tour of the neighborhood with us. Since he still had his keys, the truck must be close by. As we made our way to the adjacent street, we spotted his truck. Given all the stress, Mike wasn't thinking straight, so when we yelled, "Those bastards stole your truck!" he jumped out of our car and was ready to go bang on the door. I wish we would have let those events play out, but being fearful of an interaction with an angry dad, we fessed up right then and there.

[Mike Jones with his truck circa 1992]

CHAPTER

You Don't Even Know Me!

It was summer of senior year. Kelly's parents were out of town so Omar, David V., Tony, and I were over at his house just goofing off. I think we went to the movies with a larger co-ed group earlier that night but went back to Kelly's house to play pool and hang out and eventually crash there for the night. Omar and Kelly worked at Wet N Wild, which was the precursor to what is now Hurricane Harbor. They had the early shift the next day, so they went to bed around midnight.

Tony, David, and I played pool for an hour before we grew restless. We had never tried the shaving cream trick where you would place shaving cream on a sleeping victim's hand and then tickle their nose, hoping they would give themselves a face full of Barbasol.

Omar was sleeping in an extra bedroom, and he was our first target. We crept down the hall with the can of shaving cream and opened the door as quietly as we could. We were instantly greeted by Omar yelling, "Get the @*$# out!"

We scampered down the hall, giggling like little girls. The only thing left to do was to give it one more shot with Kelly.

We were able to get close enough to start dispensing the shaving cream on his hand when he woke up. He was frustrated, but in control, and he quickly put an end to the mischief. He gathered up the pool cues, letting us know fun time was over and it was time to call it a night.

The three of us parked in Kelly's living room, ready to discuss what went wrong, when Kelly came back down the hall at a quickened pace with a look in his eyes that could send chills down Ted Bundy's spine.

There must have been some shaving cream that got on his bed. When he lay back down on it, he lost it. His only words as he entered the living room were, "Clean that shit up!"

David told Kelly we would indeed clean it up but to stop ordering us around. Suddenly, Kelly turned into the bionic man and in one motion had jumped over his coffee table, landed on David, and began to strangle him.

At one point he had hollered, "You don't even know me!"

After the chaos had stopped and Kelly returned to bed, the three of us decided we should leave. I mentioned to Tony and David that I don't blame Kelly for being so upset.

"It's 2:00 a.m., we are in his house, and we don't even know the guy," I said.

We suppressed the laughter and left. Tony's parents were also out of town. We thought it would be easier to crash there than try to sneak back into our own homes at that hour.

Tony lived in a new subdivision across town where the lots were large, and the houses were significantly bigger than the rest of our homes. As we went in the house, Tony was certain he had seen a shadowy figure moving quickly across the upstairs hallway. The next hour was a series of comical events that included everything from yelling out, "We know you are in here," to contemplating calling the cops, to thinking about leaving.

We ultimately settled on a plan of grabbing steak knives and performing a thorough search of the house. Nobody else was in there, and it was with some level of embarrassment that I say we were still a little freaked out. By now, it was 4:00 a.m. We decided to take the recliners and couches in the living room, so if the killer attacked one of us then the other two could quickly help.

As we steadied ourselves for some sleep, we all agreed that although there was a chance there was a killer in the house, we knew for sure there was one back at Kelly's place.

CHAPTER

BE CAREFUL WHAT YOU SAY

M y high school nights in Mansfield consisted of four basic events:

1. A party or school event
2. Going out with my girlfriend
3. Working
4. Figuring it out

It was the fourth option that was the basis for most of the stories in this book. A big part of this option was grabbing some buddies and driving past the 7-11 on Walnut Creek and 287 at least a few times throughout the night. There was always a reasonable chance that another group had the same idea and occasionally, we would run into others and hear about a party that popped up.

One night, Fred, Mark, Dave, Joe and I were in the Brandenburg's van heading back from something when we hit the red light on Walnut Creek and Country Club. There were 5 trucks and about 20 teenage guys at the 7-11 that we didn't recognize. It was odd that we didn't know them because our entire senior class was only 300 kids, and we knew most of the juniors.

Mark couldn't help himself, so he yelled something out the window at this group of strangers. The first attempt to get their attention was fairly innocuous, and they replied with the ever classic, "What did you say?"

That was when Mark took his game up a notch and launched the chaos that became this story... He said something rather offensive, and they scattered like ants. We told Fred to punch it and before long, we were speeding down Country Club Dr. with five trucks close behind.

The obvious issue was we had a van so there was no chance of us losing or out maneuvering them. We turned into the Brandenburg's neighborhood, all shouting different directions at Fred who was behind the wheel. On one hand, we could try to make it all the way to their house and maybe the presence of Mr. Brandenburg and the threat of calling the cops might cause them to leave. On the other hand, they would then know where we lived, and we might be inviting damage to the house on a later visit.

Before we could figure out the best plan of action, we had been boxed in by a truck passing us and hitting the breaks. One pulled up beside us, one was at our rear, and a couple others were behind them.

To our right, was the front yard of some unknown homeowner. Since we were outnumbered 4 to 1, we decided not to get out and start swinging. We kept the doors locked, and they started kicking the van. By a stroke of luck, we did have a small (little league) Louisville slugger in the van for some unknown reason.

Mark eventually opened the side door of the van with bat in hand. The most aggressive of the assailants were still close to the opening, looking for an opportunity to drag Mark out of the van which would have spelled disaster. Mark did strike one blow to his leg and one stranger connected a boot to Mark's sternum. So far, it was a draw.

One of our favorite parts to this story was one of the other guys was right outside the passenger side staring at Dave who was riding shotgun. He would reach his hand through the open sliding door where Mark was at a standstill with the couple of thugs who were ready to make a move. He would attempt to reach into the front seat to manually unlock the passenger door. He wanted to open it from the outside in order to drag Dave out. Dave was able to quell his efforts by girl-slapping his hand away.

It turned out that this group of kids was from the neighboring town of Kennedale. I'm not sure what prompted it, but the truck immediately behind us had left and Fred recognized the window of opportunity. He jammed it in reverse, went partially up into the unknown homeowner's yard, flipped it in drive, and we were back out and running with the trucks in chase once again.

We went back toward the scene of the original verbal altercation, but this time luck was on our side. A police officer pulled behind us, and it was between us and the first truck in pursuit. The officer flipped on his lights, and we pulled through the intersection of Country Club and

Walnut Creek and into a grocery store parking lot which was closed at that hour.

I believe that grocery store has long since been turned into a 24 Hour Fitness. As the cop came up to question Fred, all five trucks headed East on Walnut Creek toward the high school — no doubt they went the back way to 287 and back to Kennedale. Fred explained in three sentences that those trucks had been chasing us. The officer commanded us to stay put as he got in his car and went after them.

While we sat in the parking lot waiting for the officer to return, Joe astutely told Mark to get rid of the bat. Mark went to the edge of the parking lot where it was just a drop-off with nothing but trees and a creek and tossed the bat into the darkness. A bit later when the officer returned, he said the other group had mentioned being assaulted with a bat and asked to search the van. We quickly obliged, but with no evidence to support their claim, he let us go and returned his attention to them.

We never found out if they faced any consequences and for a brief period of time, we had thought about rallying our numbers and settling the score. However, those desires quickly faded and, in the end, a small dent to the van was the only lasting physical piece of evidence from an otherwise eventful evening.

[Not the night in question but Fred with the only picture of the van we could find]

CHAPTER

ROAD SIGNS

would imagine that taking road signs is an American tradition performed by teenagers across the country. Those signs are then used to decorate bedrooms or other hangouts.

These two short stories are a bit different.

When we were juniors, there was a senior on the football team who used to throw parties on a regular cadence. I'm not sure what his parents did or where they went off to, but it seemed like Jesse had the run of the house an awful lot.

At one party, Dave had dabbled a bit much in whatever the drink was for the night and was primed for trouble. We didn't drink much in high school and were learning that Dave was especially susceptible to suggestion in an inebriated state.

We turned his energy toward the stop sign at the end of the street. It was just sitting there, almost mocking him. How could any self-respecting varsity football player allow that stop sign to stay where it was, commanding vehicles to stop by its mere presence?

We were just about to convince him that he couldn't take that thing down when he launched into a full sprint and tackled the stop sign with such form and force that it would have made Coach Cooley proud. He had successfully taken the sign down but sliced his thumb wide open in the process.

None of us had any experience with bandaging wounds. Ian already knew he was a future soldier and was pretty much up for any challenge. He took a closer look at the wound. Although it was a candidate for stitches, none of us wanted to leave the party and we were scared to take Dave anywhere in his current condition. Ian engineered some makeshift wrap to stop the bleeding, and I have to say he did a decent job.

Dave's favorite part of the story is what happened the next day.

About half of our crew played on the high school basketball team. The rest of us were football players and enjoyed playing for the Mansfield rec basketball league (MYB) every year. We had games the next day, and with a hangover and a thumb still held together with a ripped T-shirt impersonating a bandage, Dave went for 20 and had his best game of the year.

That same year, we had one other run-in with road signs. Before Dave's parents bought him the Jeep, he drove a small yellow used pickup. One night at the Brandenburg's, Cade, Dave, and I wanted to set barricades in the hallway outside of Mark's bedroom. We knew just where to go to get the necessary materials too. There was a new construction zone across town toward Ragland road.

We set out to grab some of the road blockades with the yellow blinking lights. After we had nabbed one, the biggest test was transporting it back to their house without getting pulled over. We couldn't figure out how to turn off the light, so we traversed the entire town with that yellow blinking beacon calling attention to us. Thank goodness it was late and we didn't see anyone on the return trip.

Once back in the neighborhood, we dropped off the barricade and went back out for a stop sign to complete the ensemble.

Now that we had what we needed, we simply put it outside of Mark's bedroom just to piss him off when he woke up the next morning.

It had the intended effect.

CHAPTER

WRECKED THE VET

Joe's dad had a red Corvette that was absolutely awesome. By the time we were seniors, he was letting Joe take it out more. We always felt a little cooler on the nights where we were in the vet with the top off, cruising around town.

Stop me if you've heard this before, but one random night, Joe and I were out in the vet with nothing planned. We were cruising by 7-11. On this particular pass, we saw Megan and Jennifer coming out and stopped to ask them if they had heard of anything going on.

Besides 7-11, the other spot that provided occasional luck was the Arbors. It was an undeveloped community off of East Broad Street where we would sometimes gather for impromptu parties. It was a hotbed of activity the previous year, but the class of '91 overused it and the cops were usually quick to shut it down.

Megan, Jennifer, Joe, and I decided we would go check it out and worst case, the four of us could hang out on the dark streets of the unsuccessful development.

Current day: If you go on East Broad from 287, you'll see commerce, wide roads, stop lights, and everything else you get with a developed community. In 1992, it was a two-lane road with a perfect S curve with farmland on each side. As we turned on East Broad, Joe slowed down to let the girls get way ahead of us.

When I asked him what he was doing he said, "I'm going to show you the turns of your life."

When you are headed east, the first part of the S curve is the left turn. I'm not sure how fast we were going, but I know it was 50 something. The vet had a digital speedometer that I had never seen before. From my vantage point, I could only see the first digit on the dash.

Rather than cutting the curve and going into the on-coming lane, Joe remained disciplined in the outer lane as the vet hugged the road like the American muscle car it is. It was truly impressive.

As we straightened and began to enter the right turn portion of the S curve, we saw the taillights from Megan's car fast approaching. I quickly thought that our only safe course was to go to the oncoming lane, pass them, and then fall back to the right lane as we reduced to normal speed. Joe may have had the same thought but through instinct, he touched the breaks ever so slightly. Given our rate of speed and the fact that we were still negotiating the curve, we began a spin. It happened so quickly. I can't say we knew exactly what was going on, but I do remember looking out the window and seeing grass. I was certain we were well off the road.

After the collision with an unknown object, Joe asked if I was okay and amazingly, we both were fine. We had ventured at least 20 yards off the road, and the rear passenger side of the car had completely crumbled around a telephone pole.

One thing that stuck out to me was the reaction of his parents, Ray and Mary. As they arrived, we were waiting for the police. They were strictly worried about our wellness and handled the situation with a calming and comforting presence that I still remember.

Although shaken, we both walked away with minor scrapes and stiffness but no serious injuries. The vet, however, was beyond repair. The back of it looked like a crushed coke can and was totaled at book value.

A Corvette is just too much car for a high school kid.

[Joe with the vet sometime our senior year]

CHAPTER

10

LETHAL WEAPON

The scene was Sunday night open gym at the Methodist church. The crowd was light that night and for some reason, I remember that the games were competitive with a better quality of play than usual. It was summer, so we had some flexibility to do something afterward but there really wasn't anything on the docket.

David V., Mike, Kelly, and I were sitting on the stage cooling down from the action. David began to explain that his cul-de-sac had been victim to a few car break-ins where the thieves were settling for audio equipment and loose change in the consoles. Based on what they had stolen, it was determined that they were probably no good kids.

Mike was going back to David's house so they could sit up on the roof with paintball guns to wait for the burglars. Kelly and I gave each other a knowing glance. We weren't sure how we could capitalize on this new information, but we knew we'd come up with something.

In the parking lot, Kelly and I had decided we would run home to shower, put on some dark clothing, and then go to Vaillancourt's house to impersonate the robbers.

I picked Kelly up thirty minutes later, and we parked a couple blocks over from David's house. We were walking through his neighborhood, finalizing the plan. Despite it being summer, we wore dark sweatshirts for extra cushion from the pending paintball attacks and wore hats that were pulled down low to act as both a disguise and protection. I can't remember what the upside was to our plan outside of a laugh but the downside was a paintball to the face.

David's cul-de-sac was not a traditional long road ending in a circle. It was basically a semi-circle cut out of the adjacent road, so all five houses shared the one large opening. This meant that we were at risk of being spotted as soon as we entered the area which would have been a good 25 yards from David's house.

Kelly and I walked with purpose to David's Jeep Cherokee which was parked in the driveway. We didn't think we saw them up on the roof as we approached, but we didn't dare look directly up for fear of being outed and fear of a shot to the eye.

David left his doors unlocked on purpose to lure the criminals into their plan. Kelly and I had spent the better part of two minutes grabbing and throwing cassette tapes, loose change, and making far more noise than necessary to try and garner some sort of reaction but to no avail.

As we had lost interest and were walking away at the end of his driveway, David burst out of his front door doing his best Mel Gibson impression. It was obvious he hadn't cleaned up yet because he was still wearing his basketball shorts, but he had no socks, no shoes, and no shirt on. He would have clearly been refused service at any respectable establishment in his present condition. He was also carrying his paintball semi-automatic weapon that resembled an AK-47.

He hollered, "Get back here you little bastards!" and began to take off after us.

David played basketball and was quick on the court, but he was never a threat to win a footrace. The fact that Kelly and I had a twenty-yard head start and a speed advantage allowed us to pull clear of our tracker by the time we were two streets over. We hid in some bushes and watched David continue his pursuit as he passed by. Just as we were about to work our way back to the car, we heard the sirens and saw the flashing lights of a police officer entering the neighborhood at a high rate of speed, no doubt looking for the same hoodlums David was chasing. We ducked back down and let the officer pass us. It turned out Mike, who was still back at the Vaillancourt's home, had called 911 as David took off to execute his plan of doling out justice the good old fashioned way.

My car was on the next street over, in the opposite direction of the chase, so it would have been quite easy to slip away into the night and get back home with no additional drama. That was my vote as we could then gather with our other cronies the following day to listen to the heroic tale of how Mike and David were standing up to the rising crime problem in Mansfield. I could almost see it playing out where Kelly and I would ask questions and get them to expand on this unlikely tale before finally busting out laughing and sharing the real news.

As I was playing out that scenario in my head, Kelly brought me back to earth and explained that we better go fess up now and straighten things out with the police. He said that my car was parked on the adjacent street, and if anyone noticed and the cops ran plates and figured out it was my car in David's neighborhood, then we might be in big trouble.

In retrospect, that was giving the neighbors and Mansfield's finest far too much credit but it made sense at the time. We worked our way back near David's house where we saw two police officers talking to Mike and David. The sirens were now silent, but the lights were still flashing. We walked up slowly and began to explain the situation.

When we originally planned this prank, I couldn't wait to see the look on their faces when we revealed that we were the bad guys, but the current circumstances took all the laughter and fun out of what would have been a glorious moment.

After hearing us out, the police officers informed us that they would be taking Kelly and me into the station. David very calmly explained to them that he was not pressing charges when the officer more emphatically explained back to him that it wasn't David's call. That was when one of the officer's put it in terms that we clearly understood and shocked us back into reality.

First, they had responded to a 911 call and sped across town putting themselves and others at risk of the high-speed response.

Second, and more importantly, as they entered the area, they saw David coming around the corner with what looked like an automatic weapon. They explained that he was very lucky they didn't blow him away right then and there. I've had horrible thoughts about all that could have gone wrong over the years and felt incredibly lucky that it was only an amusing tale we rarely reference.

I don't know if the officers knew it wasn't worth their time to bring us in or maybe they realized that they actually did scare us straight, but after another five minutes of conversation, we were free to go.

Kelly, if you are reading this, we missed the payoff. If we would have left quietly, we could have let Mike and David bask in their glory for several days before finally busting them at the right moment in front of mixed company.

CHAPTER

MAKESHIFT MINI GOLF

Same story, different night.

Joe, Dave, David V., Fred, and I were out messing around with no real plans. One thing that we did very infrequently, and usually with female companionship, was go to the Putt Putt off I20 and Cooper St in Arlington. Not only was it a great place for a date, but it also had an arcade which included Cyberball, possibly the greatest video game of all time. I can't remember what prompted the idea, but we had thought it may be fun to see if we could get in an after hours private round of mini golf. It was summertime and a weeknight so they closed down by 9:00 p.m. and it was probably closer to midnight by the time we arrived. Like our excursions at TX Stadium, our enhanced entry technique consisted of climbing the fence.

Once we found ourselves on the property, we realized that we didn't have access to the equipment to play a round, and we were not about to break into the actual building. We may have been troublemakers, but we drew the line somewhere.

There is some level of disagreement on how it progressed from there, but I'll go with my version. Like all of us, I have more confidence in my memory than that of my friends.

For no particular reason, we began messing with one of the larger than life-size flamingos that decorated the course. Basically, with not much more than a firm push, we were able to dislodge it from the ground. We now had a 5-foot flamingo in our possession. We weren't quite sure how we would exploit this new and exciting development, but we knew whatever we did was going to be badass.

With a bit of effort, two of us lifted and handed the flamingo over the fence to the other guys who had already scaled the wall and were back on the parking lot side. David's Jeep Cherokee had a hatchback and, with some finagling, we were able to fit the lifeless bird in the back once we put the seats down. It was a crammed ride back with the now six of us in the Jeep.

After some consideration, the endgame became clearer. We would get another vehicle, like my 10-year-old Buick Regal, gather some other necessary elements, and build a makeshift mini-golf course in Corey's front yard. I can't recall why we chose Corey for this other than she was one of the more attractive girls in our school and one of the nicest people in our class. We were all friends with her, but not great friends, which somehow made the idea make more sense. If we were to pick one of our girlfriends' places or a buddy's house, it would have been obvious, and we would have been busted immediately.

After securing a couple of pins from the local golf course and a few of the mini-flags on the practice putting green, we planted the flamingo and rearranged a few of her front yard landscaping decorations. After that, we sat back and marveled at our work. It looked worthy of a $5 ticket to get in.

That's pretty much it. I'm now at the age where I'm guessing her father was when we pulled this stunt. I feel bad when I put myself in his shoes. If I were leaving for work one morning and saw this spectacle in my front yard, I would be more than a tad bit upset.

However, in all honesty, I'd also be a little impressed. I hope he had similar feelings.

CHAPTER

TIME FOR TONY TO COME HOME

One random weekend Joe, Dave, Mike, and I were once again running around town without a plan. Our Friend Tony was in a serious relationship with Suzanna, who was one of the quietest and sweetest girls in our school. We knew Tony was over at her house, and we didn't have anything better to do than to jack with him. We decided that we would somehow lure him out of the house and make him drive home. Since he drove a truck, two of us would be in the bed of the truck and try to scare him.

It seems odd to us now that we would want to intentionally freak out the driver of a vehicle that we were in, especially while laying loose in the truck bed. But as many stories go, it seemed like a good idea at the time...

This was before cell phones, so Dave took Mike back to his house so he could look up the number to Suzanna's residence. After that, he would place a phone call and impersonate Tony's dad, asking Suzanna's parents if they could send Tony home. While Mike was completing his end of the mission, David came back and parked one street over to monitor while Joe and I lay in the truck bed waiting for our friends to come through.

After several minutes, Tony came sprinting out of the house. A few seconds later, Joe and I were bumping along in the bed of the pickup truck as Tony was speeding toward his home.

Now that we completed the first phase, Joe and I looked at each other as if to question "what now?" We first tried subtle things to get Tony's attention, but it wasn't working. Eventually, we were beating on the back window and Tony had lost his composure. He later told us that as he adjusted his rearview mirror, he could see our tennis shoes so he knew there were two aggressors in the bed of his truck. He began driving erratically and hollering out the window that he would flip the truck and kill us.

This was when Joe and I realized that the lack of planning for this caper may have dire consequences. Before we could yell at him that it was us, he had slowed the truck down to the point where we had our window of opportunity to not only escape possible death, but also get away with our anonymity intact. We leapt out of the truck bed and began sprinting into the woods that made up much of this undeveloped subdivision.

By this time, Dave was already one street over, ready to pick us up. We could see his distinctive Jeep headlights through the trees. We made it safely out as Tony raced down the remainder of his street.

Once home, he had asked his dad why he needed to leave Suzanna's early. His dad was confused and said he didn't place the call. Tony started to piece it together and called Joe later that night. Joe confessed that it was us in the back of his truck, and we all had a good laugh.

I chalk this story up to another example where the best outcome was a decent laugh with a few friends and the worst possible outcome was death.

CHAPTER

PIZZA CHALLENGE

The summer between our junior and senior year, Dave, Joe, and I worked parking for the Texas Rangers. Dave had a typical role where you would arrive 90 minutes before the game, work until the second inning, get a meal break, and return by the seventh inning stretch to work egress until the parking lot cleared out.

Joe and I quickly became favorites of Peggy, the parking director, and scored a sweeter gig. We were assigned to the employee parking lot. We had to show up 60 minutes before everyone else and ensure that none of the employees parked in the first four rows of the lot as this would be used for overflow parking if needed. While everyone else had to work parking after the game, Joe and I were free to leave after the 1st inning. Looking back, this was completely useless because the Rangers would draw about 10K per night with the obvious exception of when Nolan Ryan took the mound. On the nights where Nolan pitched, they would draw up to 25K, but even then, we would rarely need to direct traffic to the employee lot.

We didn't complain as our duties consisted of sitting in a car, listening to music, and talking about sports and the latest happenings with the girls at school. Occasionally, we would have an employee try to slip into the first four rows. When that happened, we would put the car in gear, pull up next to them, and ask them to move back. Many of the older employees would argue with the faulty logic, but we would hold firm and if needed, bring the radio to our mouth and say "De'Verle, we have a problem in the employee lot." Once that happened, the employee would give us a few choice words and reluctantly comply. De'Verle was our supervisor. He was a great dude who provided no oversight and often showed up smelling of the lunch cocktails he had consumed which worked in our favor.

I can't remember why, but Joe was out one day and Dave and I made plans to grab something to eat during his meal break. There was a new Ci Ci's pizza down off Collins St. which fit our budget and our taste. I decided to drive because I was free to go after dinner so I would just drop Dave off back at his lot and keep going.

On the drive over, we challenged each other to see who could eat more pizza since it was an all-you-can-eat buffet. To keep things simple, all pieces counted the same regardless of toppings so we would get plates of five pieces at a time to keep the math manageable.

I could eat an embarrassing amount of food, but I was not at the top of my game that night and was feeling the cheap pizza sticking to my gut by the time I was on my second plate. Dave came back with his third plate and was going strong. It took me so long to finish my second plate that he had lost track and assumed we were tied at 15 slices each. I saw no reason to correct the count so we each returned to the buffet for another plate. I believe I was on 13 and he was on 18 when I saw the struggle in his eyes. Much like playing tic-tac-toe, we saw this as a no-win situation and agreed to call it a draw if we could stop eating right then and there.

I was hurting, but Dave was miserable. He was curled up in my Buick Regal on the drive back wondering how he would work the remainder of his shift. I dropped him off and as he began to slowly waddle back to his post, I rolled down the window and yelled, "Hey, dipshit. I only ate 13; you won!"

CHAPTER

14

LOOKING FOR EMPLOYMENT

Between football and schoolwork, my parents didn't make me get a job during the school year but I've basically had a job off and on since I was fourteen. I've done everything from working a snow cone stand to sacking groceries and lawn care before I had a license to loading trucks, work for the Rangers, and deliver pizzas. I ultimately settled into a job waiting tables and bartending every summer and holiday break in college as well as working fast food and a few other odd jobs in Nacogdoches during college.

As the school year wound down senior year, Fred and I were out job hunting. This was back before there were online applications, so we were driving around Arlington filling out paperwork at places we would be willing to work.

We were hungry but didn't have money. Creativity is often born from desperation. We were in the North Arlington area, and we knew that there were two El Chico restaurants within a few miles of each other so we were able to devise a plan that would give us enough sustenance to continue our employment search.

We went to one El Chico, asked for a table for four, ordered water, and began chowing down on the chips and salsa. I've seen my son go to town on his food, so I have a pretty good idea of what Fred and I looked like as we scarfed down three bowls of free chips and salsa in an 8-minute span.

Once we felt like we had enough to continue job hunting, we asked the server if there was another El Chico close by.

She said, "Yes, just a few miles away."

We gave a performance worthy of joining the theater club as we argued with each other and ultimately explained to the server that our girlfriends must be waiting for us at the other location. With panic in our voices, we asked, "How much do we owe you?"

She explained we just ordered water (we were well aware) and that we should head out to try and meet them before they left. She shared our concern and wished us luck as we bolted from the restaurant with fake urgency.

I'm pretty sure we didn't leave a tip, which I'm not proud of but again, desperate times...

That same summer, Fred's twin brother, Mark, found a job at a produce market. I don't know the entire scope of his responsibilities, but I do know it involved being there at 6:00 a.m. every weekday to stock inventory. With a few weeks left in the summer, Mark had enough and decided he would terminate his employment early. The issue was he couldn't tell his parents. Mark was leaving in August to go play football at a small school in Kansas and only had a few weeks left to kill, so he asked if he could crash on my couch at 6:00 each morning until the summer ended so he could keep up the charade with his folks.

I obliged. Each morning, I would answer the door, let him in, and go back to my room to continue sleeping. The first day, I remember my dad asking me what was up with my friend on the couch. I explained the situation and he shrugged as if to say "whatever."

I don't know how Mark explained the lack of income to his parents and maybe he never did. I haven't seen his parents in years, but if I get a chance to catch up with Pat and Fred Sr., I can't wait to bust him.

CHAPTER

PARTY AT THE BURG'S

N owadays, it is more difficult for kids to throw parties when their parents leave for the weekend. We all have monitoring systems, and many adult friend groups are born from their kids' social circles, so the amount of oversight has increased considerably.

In Mansfield in the 90s, it was a foregone conclusion that someone would throw a party if their parents were gone. It was nearing the end of our senior year, and we were preparing for the party of all parties because Mr. and Mrs. Brandenburg were out of town. At first, there was some discussion about keeping it to a small and select group. We kind of ran the school by this point so we could easily get the desired co-ed crowd there and probably avoid the disasters that came with larger mobs. That plan was dismissed.

If you know Fred and Mark, they don't do things half-way. Word was out, and it was on.

In preparation for the party, Ian, Dave, and I scored a bottle of tequila. It probably involved either Ian or Cade pretending they were 21 with their larger than average frames and selecting a place that was known to be lax on carding. Although a few of these stories involve alcohol, drinking was not a big part of our high school culture. Like most towns, it showed up at all non-supervised parties, but we didn't partake in that frequently. This, however, was a special occasion.

We arrived at the Brandenburg's a good hour or two ahead of the party and decided we would pre-party by opening the tequila. As inexperienced drinkers, we made a game plan that was guaranteed to fail. It seemed sensible that we would take turns with shots every seven minutes until we had finished the bottle. We rolled dice to decide the order which was

1. Dave, 2. Inky, and 3. Ebone. The fact that it spelled out DIE should have been enough warning to reconsider, but we plowed through.

I'm sure each of us winced internally at the first couple of shots, but none of us wanted to be the first to back down. The alcohol started to really hit toward the end of the bottle, but we had almost completed the assignment, so we stuck to the plan. I was the lightweight, literally and figuratively, so I barely made my way to the couch where I proceeded to sleep through most of the party. I was out before the first guests arrived. Dave stumbled through the night knocking things and people over along his path. Ian managed to be somewhat present at the party, but his consumption caught up to him later in the night.

I have hazy recollections of waking up and seeing some of this late in the night, but most of my "memory" is from hearing the stories from the guys over the years. The party was everything it was advertised as. Eventually, there were cars parked along the entire neighborhood as hundreds of kids packed into the house, the backyard, and milled about the streets.

Eventually, the cops showed up and broke things up. It was what you would typically see in any movie about a high school party getting out of hand. In fact, word got out so much that a group of kids from Arlington showed up before the police did. I don't know why it was necessary to start fights when you had two competing high schools at the same social event, but rules are rules. We didn't make 'em, and we didn't break 'em.

A lot of tough talk turned into pushing and shoving. There were several minor altercations where girls and friends held people back. As tensions boiled, Ian found himself in a bout with one of the larger dudes from Arlington. It caught everyone's attention because they were the two biggest guys there. It was a scene to behold as all of the surrounding chaos stopped to turn the universal attention toward the key matchup.

It did not turn out well for Ian...

Every once in a while, we'd bring this story up and wonder if Ian would have been victorious if not for the tequila. Opinions vary, but the one thing we know for sure is that his fate was sealed the moment we finished the bottle.

CHAPTER

THE GRANDEST OF CANYONS

When spring break arrived our freshman year of college, we were spread out across various schools; however, most of us came back to Mansfield for the week. Joe, Omar, and Mark were out of state and had different schedules, so they were unable to join this adventure.

It was Friday night when we all returned to town and got together in the Brandenburg's front yard to scheme up a plan. It was Dave, David V., Kelly, Fred, Ian, Mike, Cade, and me. Most of us were in college. Dave was "taking a semester off" and Cade was on his way to the U.S. Army.

As we debated options, we generally agreed that it was futile to stay in town for the week. Several of the girls we hoped to catch up with would not be returning, and we were at risk of running into the high school seniors all week. It was only a year earlier when we reigned, but now we were on the verge of being those dudes who hadn't moved on.

With slim options and poor planning, the one idea that gained traction was a trip to the Grand Canyon. The plan was simple: go to the Grand Canyon, camp in the Grand Canyon, hike back up, and drive home by mid-week. Mr. and Mrs. Brandenburg had one of the old school large vans, and we thought we could pile in and go. Amazingly, they said we could take the van on one condition: We needed a second vehicle. Thank God they made that rule because fitting eight guys and luggage into that van would have made for an awful trip.

Ian drove an Isuzu Trooper that must have had 200K miles on it. His parents initially said no, but they soon acquiesced, and the plan was coming together. We agreed to meet at the Brandenburg's the next morning at 6:00 to begin the 14-hour drive to the Grand Canyon.

We planned this trip just as 18-year-old kids would... we didn't. We threw a few tents in the Trooper, we all had a backpack with a change of clothes, we bought a map from 7-11, and we were on our way. No smart phones, no GPS, no Apple Pay... just eight guys with enough money for gas and a few meals.

I don't remember a lot about the trip to AZ outside of the fact that Cade was with Ian, and most of the luggage in the Trooper and the rest of us were in the van. David, Dave, Kelly, and I were in the back of the van taking full advantage of the sophisticated AV system. Back then, a 12" TV with a VCR connection was true luxury, and we soaked it in as we watched movies while Mike and Fred navigated the journey.

We arrived at the Canyon and went straight to the top to look at the majestic chasm. Mike was our former class president and the most responsible out of us, and he soon found a park official to ask how far we could make it down before it was too dark to set up camp. As she explained, you can only stay in the canyon if you have a reservation and those require months of lead time. This was the first of many real challenges, and yet we remained undeterred.

We went just outside of town, found a back road where we drove down about a mile, and got out to assess the situation. We grabbed the tents and marched about 400 yards into the woods where we found an opening to set up camp. Amazingly, we started a fire, pitched the tents, broke out the food we had brought, and we were living it up.

After a few hours of goofing around, it was time for bed. It was around this time when we were fully realizing the second big challenge. We anticipated "chilly" but that time of year it got below freezing, and we were all tucked away for the night in 28-degree temps. If we could just make it to the next morning's sunrise, then we would be on our way to hike the Canyon.

After a couple hour nap, I was so cold that I couldn't go back to sleep. In my mind, if I could make it back to the van then it would be far warmer than the tent. I got up, found one of the flashlights, and started making my way back to the dirt road where we had parked. It was so dark, I had no idea if I was headed in the right direction and couldn't see more than ten feet in front of me even with the flashlight.

I eventually made it back to the van and climbed inside to realize it was about the same temperature inside the van. Although the van provided very little additional comfort, it was roomier and I found one item of particular interest. It was a pair of gloves that was left behind. My feet were the coldest so the next morning when the guys came back to the van, they found me reclined in the captain's chair with the gloves covering my toes.

We had survived the night, but I was quickly realizing our third big challenge. I was feeling just a bit off when we left Mansfield and knew that a cold or something was coming on. The night of camping set me over the top, and I was sicker than a dog. As we made our way to the Canyon, I was feeling a bit better. I didn't have much of an option, so I started the journey down to the bottom with the guys. There were several signs warning that visitors should not try to hike down and back up on the same day. Those signs obviously didn't apply to such accomplished athletes, so we began the journey.

We were somewhere past the half-way point when I had to admit I was in no condition to continue and would have to tap out. Dave, Fred, and Kelly stayed with me while the other four continued their hike to the bottom.

After a rest and some water, we started negotiating our way back up. If you haven't hiked the Canyon before, it can be a frustrating experience. As you near the top, it feels like you could almost throw a rock and clear the ledge. However, in actuality, you have a couple of miles of hiking left due to the grade and distance of the switchbacks. You also have to stop every five minutes to let those who rented mules pass by. During the several hour hike back up, we all decided I was too sick to camp outside again so we felt we should pool our money and get a hotel room. I could see their faces light up as they planned it. It was easy to blame it on me but the thought of a shower, a bed (even the floor), and a 72-degree room was getting everyone giddy. We eventually made it to the top and started getting excited about indoor lodging while we waited for the others.

I have to give full credit to Mike, Ian, Cade, and David V. for making it down and back in one day. We heard from the others that at one point, they started jogging on the way down, making fun of those who would be unable to complete such a mundane task. But the climb back up got even the best of us. At one point, Cade fell and started to verbally berate himself. The others were amused but dare not laugh for fear of retribution. They finally made it to the top and looked as if they wouldn't have made it even one more step. When we relayed the plan, they were even more eager than us to find a hotel room. "Inky is too sick" they all agreed, but not one person wanted to repeat the experience from the night before.

We pooled our money and found a hotel with an available room when we realized the next challenge. Hotels don't rent to 18-year-olds, and they don't take cash. They also certainly don't want eight college kids sharing a room...

I'm still fuzzy on how we overcame the basic policy, but Kelly was the only one of us with a credit card that his parents had provided. After several minutes of negotiations and the use of his older brother's ID, he had secured a room. We hit McDonalds, gathered our stuff from the campsite, and went back to the room to take turns showering. We then settled in for the greatest night of sleep we had ever experienced.

We had given Kelly most of whatever cash we had leftover to cover the hotel expense, so the ride home consisted of some gas money and just enough change for a can of soup that I ate from the can itself.

Lubbock was our last stop before returning home. It was getting dark, and we still had over four hours to go. As we were about to pile back into the vehicles, Cade grabbed Dave and stated, "You are riding with Ian." Cade then jumped in the van with us.

Back in the early 90s, we listened to country, rock, hip hop, rap or whatever but Ian was the only one of us who dabbled in heavy metal. He had a Megadeth cassette stuck in the tape player of his Isuzu. The only thing you could do was rewind it to the same side of the cassette over and over. Dave's job for the last five hours of the trip was to keep Ian awake while listening to Megadeth.

When we got back the next day, I went to the doctor and was diagnosed with bronchitis. The remainder of that spring break was spent in bed, but the memories of the Grand Canyon would last me a lifetime.

As I look back on this story, the most amazing thing was the freedom we enjoyed. That is one way to say I have no idea what our parents were thinking. Now that I have kids of that age, it is mind-boggling to think that I came home Friday evening and told my parents I'm driving with my buddies to the Grand Canyon the next morning without a thorough interrogation on plans or a check on my money situation. On one hand, it is easy to criticize their parenting skills; however, on the other hand, that freedom was the basis for these memories, this book, and these friendships that have lasted decades.

[The guys at the Brandenburg's house at 0600 ready to depart on the journey]

[Left to right: David V., Kelly, Ian, Dave, Me, Cade, Mike, Fred]

CHAPTER

BRIDGE JUMPING

This is one chapter that I will start and end with a warning to my kids or anyone else reading this book. Bridge jumping is stupid. You do not know the exact depth of the water you are jumping into, and you have no idea what lies beneath the water's surface. There could be stumps or something else that could cause serious injury or even death.

That said, we used to bridge jump. I remember Omar and I bridge jumping at least a few times off the old rail bridge at Joe Pool Lake. It was usually when we were with girls and just doing it to impress them. That bridge was only 15 to 20 feet above the water and it was a short 20 yard swim back to the rocky shore, so the risk was minimal. The most dangerous thing about this jump was cutting your feet on the rocky surface after you swam back to shore. Omar had sliced his foot open once.

A night that started with female companionship and so much promise ended with me running him to the hospital for stitches.

The memory that prompted this chapter came a few years after we graduated high school. Ian had left A&M and joined the army, and Cade was also in the service training to be an Army Ranger. However, they were home on temp leave.

Dave and I were at SFA and home for summer break and along with Kyle Johnson, the five of us went to Ian's grandparents in Ennis, TX for a reason I can't remember.

We sat in the backyard sipping on whiskey and catching up when the subject of bridge jumping came up. After some big talk, it was revealed that there was a bridge over the nearby lake in the neighboring town.

About twenty minutes later, we found ourselves standing on the bridge looking down. This was not the old rail bridge outside of Mansfield. This bridge must have been 40 feet above the lake, and the water appeared black and distant from atop the bridge. As we debated the depth of the water, Cade reminded us that he was in training for an elite military unit and that he could jump from this height and "not even get [his] hair wet." He said he would go test it out and report back. Before we knew it, he was gone in midair on his way to the lake below.

When he hit the water, I'm pretty sure his hair got wet because he disappeared for several seconds before returning to the surface to let us know that the water was warm, deep, and welcoming. Kyle and Ian took turns jumping and then it was our turn. I'm generally open to thrill-seeking events, so I was ready to go; however, I could tell Dave was more hesitant than the rest of us. We made a pact similar to ones that grade school girls would make. We decided we would hold hands, count to three, jump together side by side, and then release hands in the air. It was somewhere around two and a half when Dave jumped the gun and left the bridge, pulling me with him. I yanked my hand back but the unplanned head start gave me just enough of a forward tilt that the landing was unpleasant.

In the end, we swam back to shore, drove back to Ian's grandparent's house, and resumed our night of catching up as if we never even took the quick detour to the lake.

I'll finish where I started: Bridge jumping is stupid.

[Dave and I shortly after the successful jump into lake Bardwell]

[Kyle, me, Ian, and Cade after the bridge jump]

CHAPTER

FIVE TO A ROOM

Dave, Kelly, and I started our freshman year at UTA and were commuting from home. One of the reasons I didn't go to SFA straight out of high school was because I didn't really know what I was doing on the administration side. My parents didn't go to college, so they weren't in a position to help. They also had money concerns and thought it would be best if I could start without the expense of room and board.

It was a difficult semester. Although Dave, Kelly, and I were still in town and we connected with a couple of new friends at UTA, we were not living the college life. By the second half of the semester, I had drawn up budgets, shown my parents how much I had saved waiting tables and bartending, and presented a plan to go to SFA to start the January semester. They supported me, and I was in Nacogdoches by Jan. 1993.

Dave struggled through his first semester and took the next semester off. Dave Sr. made it easy for him. He told him to relax for the spring and by fall, he would either be back at school somewhere, beginning a trade, or in the military. Dave joined us at SFA by fall of 1993.

In 1994, Dave and I were rooming together at Wilson Hall. We had become friends with Tyler and Jeremy who lived across the hall and decided that we would take a different approach to the upcoming semester. We moved their bunk beds over to our room and set up their room with our stereo, TV, play station, and basketball goal. That room would become the game room and study room while we all four slept across the hall.

That same semester, I pledged a fraternity. Fred had been at SFA since the beginning, and he was in the Kappa Alpha frat. During the rush process, I had narrowed it down to two choices, but Fred was an easy tie breaker, so I had pledged KA. Although my roommates didn't rush, they got to know several of my pledge brothers through the process and somehow put up with me coming and going at all hours.

One of our duties as pledges was to raise the flag at the fraternity house the exact minute of sunrise each morning. All pledges must be present and on time or there would be severe consequences. One of my pledge brothers who became a good buddy was Raymond. Raymond also lived in Wilson Hall on the floor above us. I didn't have a car at SFA, so his job was to drive us in his single cab pickup every morning and my job was to wake him up in time.

My job was much harder. On the mornings where their door was unlocked, I could spend up to 30 seconds violently shaking him. On the mornings where his door was locked, I would make enemies with the entire wing by pounding on it for a good two minutes.

We had cleanup duty after a fraternity party one night, and it was especially late. Fearing he would not wake up the following morning, we agreed to drag his mattress down to the first floor and pop it on our floor in between the set of bunk beds.

After class the following day, I had to explain to Dave, Jeremy, and Tyler why Raymond's mattress was on the floor. They had gotten to know Raymond in the previous weeks, so we were all friends. Whether it was pure laziness, convenience for morning duty, or for fun, we kept his mattress in our room and slept five for the last month of the semester.

Raymond was a big dude and former linebacker at Baytown, but he was not the kind to watch a scary movie or listen to a ghost story. It was easy to unnerve him, and we couldn't stop ourselves from the free entertainment. It started playfully enough where we would say "Candyman" three times, and as soon as he would tell us to stop, Dave would jump from the bottom bunk on top of him and he would scream like a little girl. Eventually, he grew accustomed to our routine and we were forced to up our game.

I think it was Jeremy who had a mini-tape recorder that was originally purchased for recording class notes. While Raymond and I were out doing ridiculous pledge duties, the other guys had recorded several minutes of silence followed by an occasional "Raymond" in a shrill faint female voice.

We had planned it out perfectly. We said two of us had tests in our early class, so we had to go lights out at an unusually early time. It was one of the rare nights where we were all there and since Raymond and I craved sleep that semester, there were no arguments. As we all settled in, I asked David to turn the fan on. While he was up, he hit the play button on the recorder which was positioned just a couple of feet from Raymond's head.

At first, Raymond tried some small talk which was normal, but Tyler told him to shut it as he needed to get to bed. Tyler was the smallest of the crew but had no need for niceties or comradery, so when he was in a mood, we generally fell in line. But this night, he was just playing along for the punchline.

After several minutes of getting comfortable, the first "Raaaaymonnnnnd" went off and we did a great job of suppressing laughter. Raymond had asked if we heard it, and we were quick to tell him to shut it and get to sleep. I'm sure each of us was laughing, but it was dark and the hum of the fan would mask any reaction any of us might have. A few minutes later, the second eerie call came out and he shot up in his bed asking, "For real, did you guys hear that?"

We again shamed him into shutting up and laying there quietly as we awaited the third and final payoff. The first two recordings were so slight that he could almost convince himself that he was hearing things, but the third was a full-on shout recorded by a girl we knew. When the recorder finally released the audio of his name screaming in a bloodcurdling manner, he shot up and ran out the door.

I think we laughed the remainder of the night.

BEATING LYNCH MOB

I know most guys hate when other guys recall their athletic prowess from their younger days, but I couldn't resist including this one story in the book. One of the best parts about college life was intramural sports. I played it all and loved every minute of it. Basketball, softball, and flickerball were fun but flag football was my favorite. I loved Greek week with the fraternity, but my fondest memories were playing on the dorm teams with a few of my high school friends and the other guys we met along the way.

We weren't the greatest team, but we won far more than we lost. What we lacked in athleticism, we made up for with scheme and knowledge of the game. I was a subpar passer playing QB, but I was faster than most which was an easy bailout in the game of flag football. The rest of our team was made up of a couple former offensive lineman: Tyler and Dave who each went about 5'4" and other non-descript looking dudes. Most of us were decent athletes, but our appearance wouldn't strike fear in the hearts of any opponents during warmups.

The one game that we still reminisce about occasionally was a game we had against a team named Lynch Mob. This was a team made up of the SFA football players who were suspended due to grades or other issues. If you lined them up against us for a visual prediction, Vegas would have set the line around 80. To make matters worse, we had a couple of guys out and were forced to play a man short so it was seven on eight the entire game. During warmups, we were joking around and were fully resigned to the inevitable outcome.

As the game started, I realized that I was faster than most of them and could at least move around enough to gather a few first downs and avoid a complete blowout. Early in the game, we had intercepted a pass and returned it for a score, so we had a lead and the slightest sense of optimism which grew into confidence as the game progressed.

The real key to the game was the zone defense we were forced to deploy due to the disadvantage in numbers. I played safety, and we put a couple of our quicker guys at D Line to put pressure on the QB. Dave played in the middle and understood how to read the plays and take away their best options.

The best part was Danny playing corner. Danny was a former O-Lineman at Mansfield and at the time, he looked like a former O-Lineman who had stopped working out. At one point in the second half, they yelled from the sideline, "Pick on the fat kid!"

The very next play, he broke up a fourth down pass. We all took great satisfaction in that play, but Danny was especially proud and started to move around with a bit more swagger. As the game wore on and we held tight to a 6–0 lead, you could tell that the frustration was mounting on their side. One of our four interceptions finally sealed the deal as we let the clock run out with the ball in our possession.

Some random intramural game at a small college holds no weight in sports folklore, but for us, it was like winning the Super Bowl.

CHAPTER

BARK LIKE A DOG

This story involves four of my high school friends but took place late into our college years. Jason, Dave, and I went to SFA. Jason and Dave lived with Danny, and I was living with one of my fraternity brothers in an apartment behind the Nacogdoches Pizza Hut. Despite girlfriends, classes, and growing social circles, we still managed to hang out fairly frequently. Joe and Omar were at LSU, and we had decided to pay them a visit and all go to Mardi Gras.

By this time, Dave was driving the "Brahma." It was a small Nissan single cab pickup truck with a camper over the bed. We made the trip from Nacogdoches to Baton Rouge with two guys up front while Jason and I took turns riding in the bed of the truck inside the camper. We left Friday right after morning classes, so we were at Joe and Omar's apartment by late afternoon. We all headed down to New Orleans to experience Mardi Gras.

I'm glad I've been to Mardi Gras but will likely never go back. It was a sea of humanity and not the cleanest of venues, literally or figuratively. It was so packed in some areas that you could lose your group if you take one step in the wrong direction. You could be separated for hours, at least. This was back before cell phones and tracking software.

That Friday night, we lived it up. Everything from hand grenades and hurricanes at Pat O'Brien's, to beignets and hot dogs off street carts... We saw girls exposing their up tops for worthless plastic beads and all sorts of things you weren't accustomed to seeing if you grew up in Mansfield.

On Saturday, we made the drive back to New Orleans. We were all moving slower and didn't have it in us to put up with the crowds and repeat the same adventure from the night before. We called it a day by early evening and drove back to Baton Rouge.

As we settled back in at their apartment, Jason took ownership of the couch and the rest of us broke out the Dominoes. I don't know when we started playing 42, but I guess it was high school because we fancied ourselves experts by this point.

Omar broke into a bottle of Crown Royal, but the rest of us had no interest in drinking that night. We played bones literally all night long and kept the tradition of playing "bark like a dog" to put the Dominoes away as dawn was approaching. That game is basically a game of luck and bluffing to make sure you don't have the last Domino (the double blank) to put away.

Omar had consumed the entire bottle of Crown over the eight hour match and indeed was the one holding the last domino. We had decided that the loser would face the consequence of truly barking like a dog in the apartment courtyard, so Omar was waking up his neighbors at 6:00 a.m. with his best Dobermann impression.

[Jason, Omar, Dave, me and Joe at Mardi Gras that Friday night]

[Omar barking like a dog in the apartment courtyard sometime around dawn Sunday morning]

CHAPTER

THE TIME I SAW A GHOST

At one of our pledge meetings, we were informed that there had been several acts of theft and vandalism at the fraternity houses around town. As a countermeasure, the pledges were to make sure we had security coverage between the hours of midnight and 6:00 a.m. for the next couple of weeks.

As I look back, I'm certain none of this was true. This was just an additional way to stick it to pledges. It had probably been passed down from previous generations, and I'm sure we did something similar to the pledges after us. Our pledge class had 16 guys, so by the time we coupled up and assigned two-hour windows to each pair, we each only needed to cover two to three shifts over that two-week span.

Raymond and I paired up, and our first assignment was the 2:00 a.m. to 4:00 a.m. shift one weeknight. We just so happened to have a party at the house that night, so we were already up there and wide awake. Whoever drew the midnight to 2:00 a.m. shift struck gold because the party didn't wind down until sometime around 1:00 a.m. so they simply had to help clean up before taking off.

"Security duty" consisted of two guys sitting on the front porch talking about which frat members were the worst hazers. This conversation would be broken up every fifteen minutes when we performed a mandatory walk around the premises to ensure there were no threats. One person would take the 30-yard walk down the lengthy front yard to look left and right on the street. The other would take a trip around the house and look in the back yard where we had the parking lot, volleyball courts, and basketball courts.

At SFA, sorority row was a planned community with several small mansions adorning the Greek letters for each affiliation. Dozens of girls lived in each home with a house mom and all the amenities you would expect.

The fraternity houses were pieces of shit scattered across town. Ours was in a neighborhood but had just enough land and space between the adjacent houses to avoid constant calls to the Nacogdoches police.

On this night, there were still a few actives hanging around when we started our shift. However, by 2:30 a.m. it was just me and Raymond taking watch. Sometime between the 3:00 and 4:00, it was time for the walk about and it was my turn to take the front. As I walked down the yard toward the street, I looked to my left and saw a figure approaching from the darkness. I stopped a good ten yards from the street which provided about 15 yards between me and my new friend. As she came into view, I had to take a moment to process what I was seeing. She seemed to be my age or slightly older. She was impossibly pale and wearing what appeared to be a white sailor's uniform similar to what I remember seeing in the photographs from my dad's time in the navy. She also had a slight limp in her gait which confused matters even more.

Several thoughts went racing through my head. Was she in trouble? Did she attend our party earlier that evening? Did she live in the neighborhood? Why would she be walking alone at 4 a.m.? Why was she dressed in such strange attire?

It's true that the brain is the ultimate processor as I had these thoughts and several more competing for my attention in a split second.

You may have gathered by this point in the book that I've never been the kind to shy away from a situation. I wasn't easily spooked. I took midnight walks through graveyards and scary movies didn't bother me. When we had our annual Halloween tradition of going in co-ed groups to haunted houses, I was more likely to sneak ahead or stay behind the group in hopes to scare everyone than I was to pack in the middle.

Yet, at this moment, something was completely off. Right as I was about to ask her if she needed assistance, she slowly looked up at me and her face was even more pale than her body or her naval uniform. I opened my mouth with the full intent to ask her if she needed help but nothing came out. She then looked straight ahead and began her limp toward the end of the street. When you are facing the street from our front yard, you have about a 20 yard field of vision between where the trees and the natural curve of the street would block your view. She was more than halfway through my field of vision and was approaching the curve, so I tried again to call out. Not only could I not make a sound, but I couldn't catch my breath. It was as if I were drowning on dry land.

As she disappeared into the darkness, I was jogging back up to the house as Raymond was coming around the side. I could still barely summon the breath to call out his name.

He said, "Dude, you look like you just saw a ghost."

I told him I may have. I grabbed him, and we both started toward the street as I was trying to explain what had happened. We started to jog toward the end of the street. At the top of the street was a T-intersection so we knew we'd be almost on top of her based on the slow pace she exhibited. We looked left and right and even split up and walked a bit in each direction, but we saw no one.

As years have passed and I've told that story to friends, my mind comes back to two competing versions. The first version is more likely. It was simply a young woman who was strangely dressed and oddly pale. She may have been in trouble, and I didn't step up to offer the assistance she needed. I regret it every time I think back. I don't completely discount the second version because I do have some level of trust in my 19-year-old self. I've never had a feeling like that before or since.

I'm not sure what I believe when it comes to the supernatural, but at least for that night, I was convinced I saw a ghost.

CHAPTER

THE FLAGPOLE INCIDENT

I am sure SFA was no different than most colleges. Parties were not in short supply, and there were a handful each semester that you could set your watch by. In Nacogdoches, the largest party of the semester followed an event we called "Steps." At the end of rush week, all of the soon-to-be pledges would gather atop the steps at the Rusk administration building on Saturday morning. The fraternities segmented themselves in groups at the bottom of the stairs with all of the sororities and hundreds of other students congregating in the nearby street looking on.

The pledges would come out of the building in groups organized by which frat they were pledging. They would take in the glory of their future brothers at the bottom of the steps as well as all of the other observers cheering them on.

After a few moments of soaking it in, the group would sprint down the steps and into a mosh pit to join their new brotherhood with all sorts of whooping and hollering. The KAs always went last and instead of having the pledges run down, we ran up the stairs and carried them down on our shoulders. After that, everyone would race to their respective houses to party for the remainder of the day and into the next morning.

By fall of 1996, I was an upperclassman and had been through this ritual several times. This version of Steps was especially memorable. It wasn't crazy hot for a September day, Honest Mango (our favorite band) was playing tunes, and the ice tub on the deck was overflowing with cold Milwaukee's Best and Keystone Light. We were settling in for what promised to be a great afternoon.

Dave lived with Jason Verhagen and Danny Price, two of our friends from Mansfield. Although they weren't in the fraternity, they were a fixture at most of our parties and had gotten to know most of the members through me and Fred. They were there with their girlfriends, enjoying the festivities.

The KA house back then was a calamity, but it was the perfect frat house. It had a massive front yard where many wiffle ball tournaments were held. It had a sand volleyball court in the back along with a 9 ft basketball goal which allowed us to occasionally dunk during our pickup games.

The house itself was nothing more than a large common area used to host parties and chapter meetings along with two hallways that led out back with three bedrooms along each hall. We needed six residents to support the rent needed so the sitting chapter president and five lottery losers would live there each semester. The lottery losers would invariably try to bargain their way out of it with younger members through intimidation techniques or cash.

I never lost the lottery and was never tempted by these methods, so I never had to live in the house. The main draw for the parties was the large outdoor deck where a band could play and folks could gather around to enjoy the weather. The other thing that made the deck attractive was the fact that folks could climb up a ladder to sit on the one-story roof, let their legs dangle over, and watch the party below. This is how Jason spent that fateful afternoon.

There were two main ways to get down from the roof. One was you could go back down the ladder you climbed up and the second was to slide down the flagpole that was only an arm's reach from the rooftop near the front of the house.

If you chose the flagpole, the only watch out was to avoid the cleat toward the bottom of the pole. The cleat was a metal bar connected to the pole that would stick up about 3" with a 2" separation from the main pole. It was designed to wrap the rope around it to adjust the height or keep the flag in place.

Jason chose the flagpole for his route back down. There were a variety of techniques used to avoid the cleat. Personally, I would swing around to the other side of the pole and avoid it entirely. Some would make an early dismount whereas most would just slow their slide and start extending their legs and reaching for the ground when they neared the bottom.

Jason decided on a new and bold method: He went down full speed and used the cleat as the brake and his crotch as the brake pad.

It was early afternoon, and the party was in full swing when the reality of the injury was settling in on Jason. He grabbed Dave and told him they must leave immediately. When they got back to their apartment, he had asked David to look at the injury to help inspect the damage. David refused to examine his balls, but after some convincing combined with the effects of the beer, he looked and agreed to leave right then and there to get Jason to the hospital where he indeed received stitches on the most private of places.

By the following week, the rumors had spread across campus that some dude had lost his beans on the KA flagpole. Some even thought he lost his frank with 'em. There were even rumors that the testicles themselves were left hanging on the pole and a friend had to put them on ice and transport them to the hospital for an unsuccessful attempt to reattach.

I can verify that those rumors were false. Jason still has a pair, and they must work because he and his wife have four kids.

Flagpole

[KA House at SFA in the 90s]

CHAPTER

WHO IS CAPABLE OF MURDER?

Charles Hicks and I became pretty good friends early on in high school. We had a lot of interaction for a couple of reasons. One is our last names. Engstrom and Hicks put us closer together in assigned classroom seating. The other is we were both on the smaller side, so we played in the same position groups of WR and DB.

Charles and I used to joke that if you could put the two of us together, you would have a great player. He was probably the fastest kid in our grade and strong for his small frame, but he wasn't the most coordinated fella. It was a bit alarming to watch him play, or try to play, basketball and he seemed to struggle catching the football every practice.

I was faster than most but envied his speed and gave up 20 lbs. of muscle to him. However, I had more coordination and found it easier to catch the football. Ultimately, the coaches placed him at DB and me at WR which was fine with me because at my size and strength (or lack thereof), I had no interest in tackling varsity running backs.

Charles was also almost a year older than me so he was driving as a sophomore and would often give me rides home from practice or to summer workouts. He drove this old beaten down truck and one of his favorite things to do was to drive on the backroads of Mansfield after dark without his lights on. There were stretches of road on the west side of town that I wasn't familiar with and when we were passing under the overhanging trees at night without headlights, we couldn't see anything. I was scared the few times we did that but I didn't want to show any fear, so I never said a word.

Although we remained tight during football season, we hung out less and less as we got into our senior year and lost touch after graduation.

It was years later when he dropped by the house one summer. I can't remember if I was still in college or had recently graduated college and was living back at my parent's house. I do know we were in our early twenties.

My mom was pleased as she hadn't seen him in years, and I was touched by the gesture of his visit. He had gotten into body building and was showing us pictures of his competitions. I thought it was a bit odd that the three of us were at my kitchen table looking at pictures of him in a speedo all oiled up, but it was good to catch up regardless. We spoke on the phone one time shortly after that but then lost touch for a second time, and I never spoke to him again.

It was several years after that when I was stranded in Charlotte on business due to some airline issues when Dave called. He had asked me if I had heard about Charles and said that he had been arrested for murder in Pennsylvania. Keep in mind that half of what Dave and I say to each other is meant to elicit a laugh, so it took a few minutes for me to realize he was serious.

It was years after that when it finally went to trial and in 2014, he was found guilty of murder and dismemberment. He was also tied to unsolved murders in Tarrant County, TX but to be honest, I haven't done much research nor do I care to. The details are very dark so rather than include them here, you can google if you want to learn more.

I think people who know people who were convicted of heinous crimes often wonder if they could see signs of it back when they knew them well. My friends and I sometimes talk about it, but to be honest, I never saw anything in the younger Charles that would ever lead me to believe he was capable of murder.

[#20 Dave Jimenez; #50 Fred Brandenburg; #23 Jose Amaya; #26 Charles Hicks; #42 Mark Brandenburg; #87 Mike Engstrom]

CHAPTER

Drafting is a Contact Sport

I can't recall the exact year, but we were probably in our mid-thirties. We changed it up that year and had draft weekend at White Bluff near Lake Whitney. We rented out a couple of the condos the developers used when they hosted prospective property buyers.

It was perfect because the condos were across the street from the clubhouse and backed up to the 18th green, so once we finished with Friday's round, we were home and ready to settle in for the night.

The routine is consistent and proven. We'd play golf, go to our place of lodging, hit a pool or the lake to cool down, and then begin to cook and drink beer. Early evening, we begin the draft, which takes painfully long, and then maybe fit in a game of poker or two before guys start disappearing off to bed.

Saturday morning, we'd wake up, cook breakfast, and go to the lake to spend the afternoon either on the boat, at a sandbar, or floating in the lake with life jackets. We occasionally have a couple of boat owners show up with their boats, but usually, we'd rent a pontoon and all pile in for the day. The second night, we repeat the process with dominoes and poker, but bedtime usually comes a couple of hours earlier than it did on Friday.

Danny is one of my best friends and my nemesis all in one. Although it's generally done in good fun, we have pushed each other's buttons over the years on everything from logistics for draft weekend to bantering about our favorite sports teams.

During this weekend, Cade made the rare appearance. He wasn't in our league but joined us for the weekend of fun. He had told Danny a couple of times on Friday that he shouldn't put up with my crap so by Saturday night, Danny was primed for conflict.

About half the group decided to go back out to the lake for a night run on Cade's boat while the rest of us stayed back and continued our poker game. I was getting up to go to the fridge and gave Danny a love tap on the back of the head. Between the gentle smack and the verbal jabs the night before, he had lost it. I was in the skinny hallway with my back turned to the guys when I heard Joe say, "Danny, no!"

Before I could understand what the comment meant, I felt a push from behind and found myself stumbling into the wall where I went shoulder first through the sheetrock. No additional activities or fisticuffs. We actually handled it reasonably well, and I accepted his apology. We resumed the poker match without another word. The incident had dampened the mood to the point where the other guys had inquiries upon their return even before they noticed the dented wall.

When I returned home the next day, I was in the game room playing with my kids who were very young at the time. I knew then that something was wrong with my shoulder. I felt extremely guilty coming back after draft weekend and then departing to the 24-hour clinic, but I had to. It was determined I had a hairline fracture, so I basically just needed to wear a brace and minimize motion for several weeks.

That Sunday morning on the drive back will forever be known as the "Whataburger incident." I had driven that weekend and had Ian, Joe, and Dave with me. We made it all the way back to the Whataburger in Mansfield before stopping for breakfast. Most of us were putting away a couple of taquitos, but Ian had stepped up his game and went full on burger meal. Whataburger on Sunday mornings was a busy place, and there was one table of older gentlemen who you could tell have a Whataburger coffee routine that they never deviate from.

After we finished, we started heading out when Ian said he needed to hit the bathroom. The three of us waited for what seemed like an eternity in my Tahoe where we could see inside the Whataburger glass windows. My shoulder ached, and I was getting impatient. Based on the time he was taking, we knew Ian was taking care of some serious business in that bathroom. One of the older gentlemen, probably 75 or 80, came out of the bathroom and walked at a quickened pace to get outside. Even out in the fresh air, he was waving his hand in front of his face as if he were swatting bees, but he was unable to distance himself from whatever he smelled moments earlier. Right on cue, Ian came strutting out of the bathroom like a peacock.

We didn't witness anything bad happen to the old man but over the years, we reached a conclusion that it was at least possible, if not probable, that he was so disoriented from sharing the bathroom air with Ian that he stumbled out onto business highway 287 where he was hit by an oncoming car. It's become an accepted fact by other league members that Ian is likely guilty of involuntary manslaughter.

CHAPTER

25

SINKING THE TITANIC

We have spent more drafts at Lake Granbury than anywhere else. It's only an hour or so from DFW, there is a golf course and Whataburger directly on the drive there, and the house is functional. It has a large living space to host the draft, a good table for poker, ample sleeping space for twelve guys, and most importantly, a boat dock.

On Friday after golf, we will get in the lake for a couple of hours to cool down and usually a few games of Dominoes will break out on the dock table. As early evening approaches, we would settle into our spots to organize our draft materials. I still bring an old school magazine because occasionally, the Wi-Fi will be spotty and I still enjoy scratching names off of a list.

Several years back, Danny reverted to the old school and started putting up the official draft board with sheets of stickers for all draftable players that you could peel and place on the board.

The Sacko (previous year's last place finisher) performs the task known as "sticker bitch." In case it's not intuitive, that person must place the stickers on the draft board when each player makes their selection. To add a bit of insult, that person would wear a men's small t-shirt that is entitled Sacko. Nobody in our league belongs in a size small.

After a night of drafting, poker, and stories, we wake up the next morning ready to get breakfast and load up a boat for a day on the lake. Over the years, we've had guys like Joe, Cade, and Dax bring their own boats but we usually rent a pontoon. We would lazily cruise around the lake, occasionally stopping to put on life vests to float in the water for a bit or find a sandbar.

This was only five or six years ago but on that weekend, we were wondering if we would even get out because Lake Granbury was so low. The marina was renting pontoons but said we must stay inside the buoys due to the water levels. Each year, a different guy will reserve the rental but usually Danny would captain the boat just as he did this year.

We were not more than a few hundred yards off the marina when we ran over a stump. In Danny's defense, he was within the defined waterway but it was difficult to see what lay beneath the surface. As we got to our first stopping point, several guys entered the water and grabbed a beer. Joe, our most seasoned sailor, was investigating and soon declared that the boat was taking on water and we needed to begin our return journey immediately. A few doubted but we fell in line. I think the 30-year-old versions of ourselves would have pushed it, but we were now older and wiser.

While we were discussing, the rain began to fall and that helped sway the votes of those who may have held out. Joe was right. By the time we were approaching the marina, the back of the boat was taking on water at a pretty good rate. There was no way we would have made it back if we had waited much longer.

We had called ahead to let them know the situation, and they had someone waiting on the dock to guide us in. We approached the dock, and Danny was ready to pull alongside and cut the engine just like he had done a hundred times.

I'm not sure if it was the weather, the bourbon from the night before, the fact that we were taking on water, or all of the verbal help we were providing, but instead of slowing, he hit the throttle. We banged into the dock with enough force to send us all around the pontoon and send the dock worker stumbling backwards.

The moment was not lost on us. We knew there were minor injuries and financial penalties coming for all of us, but we didn't care. We had just witnessed an act that would allow us to make fun of Danny at every draft for the rest of our lives.

CHAPTER

For my last story, I'm going to go all the way back to the beginning where it all started.

When I moved to Texas the second time, I didn't realize that 9th grade was high school. That made me even more uneasy but one advantage I had was that football started two weeks before classes which allowed me to meet some guys before the official school year began.

If you love football, then moving to Texas is like a Mormon moving to Salt Lake City. Even though I didn't know a soul, I was excited to join the team. It was one of my football coaches that turned "Engstrom" to "Inky" one day in practice. By the time school started, the other players were already calling me Inky and it stuck. I went through my entire high school career as Inky, and it's a name my buds still use to this day.

By 10th grade, Dave and I quickly settled into a routine where I would ride his bus home with him on Fridays and we would play basketball in his driveway until all hours of the night. I remember one particular weekend when Sandra and Dave Sr., his parents, had family in town from San Antonio and they were all going to a Rolling Stones concert in Dallas. His parents knew we were too lame to throw a party and too young to drive so they had no worries about leaving us with the run of the house.

My birthday was late August so I was several months younger than most of my classmates. David's birthday was in June, so he was in the same boat. We hadn't even begun driver's education yet, but we decided we would do what any good 15-year-old boy would do: take the Saab out for a spin. Now we weren't that crazy. We were not planning to go to downtown Fort Worth or race on the streets. We simply wanted the adventure of cruising around the neighborhood and maybe a quick run through a local drive-thru.

Dave and Sandra had a house with a two-car garage with a brick partition in the middle, so each car had to be pulled in with little room to spare. As we grabbed the keys to the Saab and entered the garage, we quickly noticed a big problem. His aunt Elsa's Camry was in the driveway behind the Saab. To this day, I don't know if Dave and Sandra did that intentionally or if it was an accidental prevention mechanism, but it represented a significant challenge regardless.

To his credit, Dave was undeterred. He said he would simply perform a series of short movements backwards and forwards and ultimately exit out of the other side of the garage. Having little to no driving experience myself, I thought it sounded plausible.

Fast forward 30 minutes and the car was completely sideways in the garage. At one point, we were both practicing deadlifts on the rear bumper to see if we could somehow lift the car and scoot it in either direction. Surprisingly, that didn't work. We must have brainstormed for ten minutes on the story we would work up before his parents came home but then decided the best course of action was to keep at it.

I was riding shotgun for the world-record 189 point turn as we painfully inched in all directions. After he resumed his efforts for another 20 minutes, the car was reasonably close to its original position. As we returned inside, dejected, he went to hang the keys in their normal place when we noticed his aunt's purse hanging on the key rack. Hanging over the side of the purse, in plain sight, were the keys to the Camry. By that time, we were so frazzled from the events of the last hour that we weren't thinking clearly. Instead of moving the Camry and taking the Saab out, we took his aunt's sedan out for a spin.

Worried about the gas gage busting us by showing the 0.5 gallon of gas we used, we decided to stop and put a few dollars into the tank. It took us several minutes to figure out how to perform the task, and we thought we'd been busted for sure by the attendant watching us fumbling around. We finally deciphered the code and put in $5 which basically topped the car off. Elsa may have been on to us when she saw the reading of the completely full tank but never outed us.

I want to thank you for going down memory lane with me. I had fun writing these stories and clarifying some of the details with the other guys.

This book was written for a very small target audience, so if you don't know me or these characters, then I want to especially thank you for taking the time to read it.

I'll close with a quick profile on each member of "The Old Mansfield Boys Fantasy Football League."

Dave Jimenez

Dave is a founding member of the league. He caught lightning in a bottle in 2007 when Tom Brady and Randy Moss tore the league up but that remains his only fantasy football title.

Ian Martin

Ian is a founding member and the gorilla of our group. Any of his group posts are immediately followed by 8 gorilla gifs. He won one fantasy football championship 20 years ago and is far more likely to win the sacko each year than his next title. He has mayoral aspirations and has asked me to serve as his campaign manager.

Joe Thomas

Joe is a founding league member and has won 7 fantasy titles including the latest controversial split championship with me when the Bills / Bengals game was called in the first quarter. The league has voiced displeasure with what was obviously my title, but compromise is part of advanced society. The 7 chips are by far most among league members.

Danny Price

Danny is one of the founding members. The rest of us drew great pleasure in the fact he had never won a championship, but he ruined our fun about five years ago when he won back-to-back titles.

David Vaillancourt

David is my dominoes partner at draft every year where we mop the floor with the other teams in several matches of 42. David has won 1 championship but usually puts together a solid team. Because he has 3 runner up finishes, he somehow thinks that should be counted when determining a team's legacy.

Fred Brandenburg

Fred has won one championship which is still a mystery because he spent that draft night drunk and verbally berating us because we were annoyed at the time it took for him to make each selection. At one point, he was studying his magazine intently for at least three minutes when I went over and realized his magazine was upside down and he was staring at an advertisement. His head is larger than most heads. I'm not referencing ego, but the physical size of that melon.

Mark Brandenburg

Mark has somehow won two championships despite being one of the worst drafters in our league. He has finished near the bottom every year outside of his two amazing runs. He is the Eli Manning of the Old Mansfield Boys FF League. Mark's specialty is using our group post to make us laugh and feel bad about ourselves at the same time.

Jason Verhagen

PCHOP joined our FF league about ten years ago when another league member left. He has yet to win a championship but does have a Sacko to his credit. Despite being a subpar fantasy football player, he is an excellent walker.

Kevin Romary

Kevin was on our high school golf team. He usually wasn't on our high school adventures which is why he wasn't mentioned in the book, but he is a long-time friend and member of our fantasy league. He has been an on-air and off-air fixture in the Lawrence, KS sports media market for a couple of decades and introduced me to Bill Self when I stopped by to visit him. Kevin lives in Lawrence with his wife and son. He is an above average fantasy player, and his name is twice etched on our mug of champions.

Anson Gordon

Anson was class of 93, a year behind us, which is why we wasn't included in our high school stories, but he's been a good friend for a long time and a fixture in our league. He lives near Austin, TX with his wife Shelby and his boys Ethan and Dillon. Anson is not only the worst fantasy player in our league but possibly America. He once went through a three year stretch with winning two games. He is 6' 5" and built like an NFL defensive end so it's extra funny when he has to wear the small size sacko T-shirt on draft night. Even though we have a random draw for draft order, he picks 12th every year.

David Harper

David was also class of 93 which is why he was absent in the book. Even though he was a year behind us he was the starting QB when I was a senior. Since I played WR, we became good friends. David joined our league a few years back when we had an opening and has yet to win a championship. We've had a few guys from the 93 class in the league over the years and they have never threatened to win a title. What he lacks in drafting ability, he more than makes up for with lake IQ and the ability to effectively transport coolers.

Dax Pemberton

Dax is class of 93 and the only member I mention that isn't in the book or officially in our fantasy league. He is assistant general manager for Mark's franchise. We hold out hope that he will one day be ready to run his own team if one of us dies or gives up. He usually takes over drafting for Mark around round 7 when Mark has either lost interest or had too much to drink. He brings his boat to draft every year, but it is only operational about 50% of the time. Dax owns a winery in Granbury, TX and practices realty.

Mike Engstrom

I am a founding member and have won four fantasy championships, second only to Joe. I have never won the sacko trophy.

Pics from the years.

Pics from the years.

[Graduation]

[The guys in Vegas circa 2001]

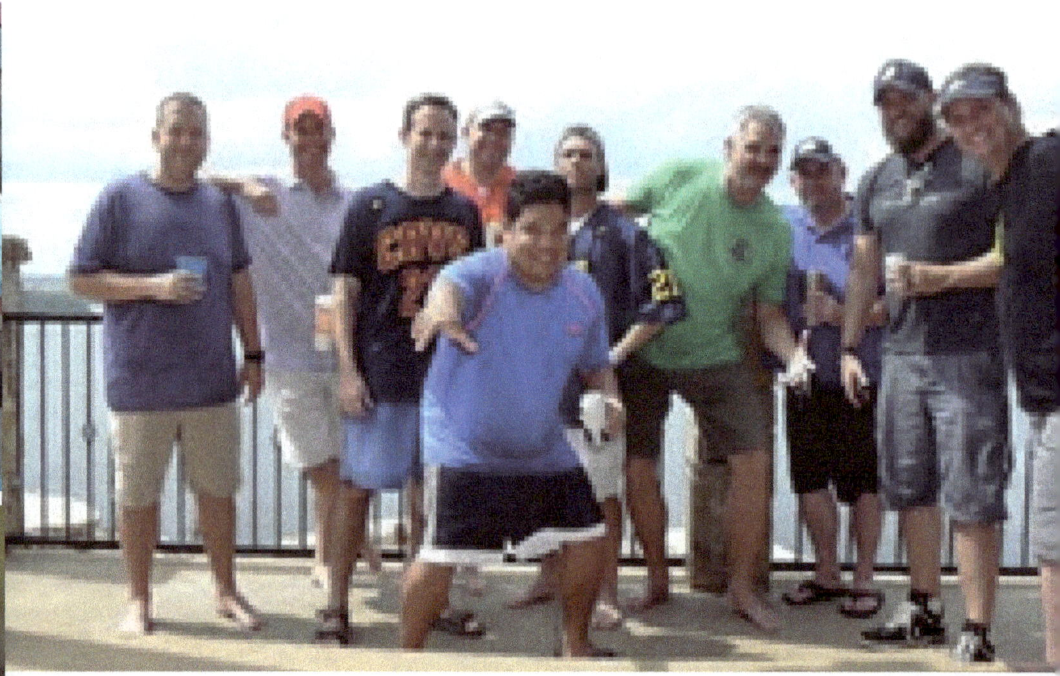

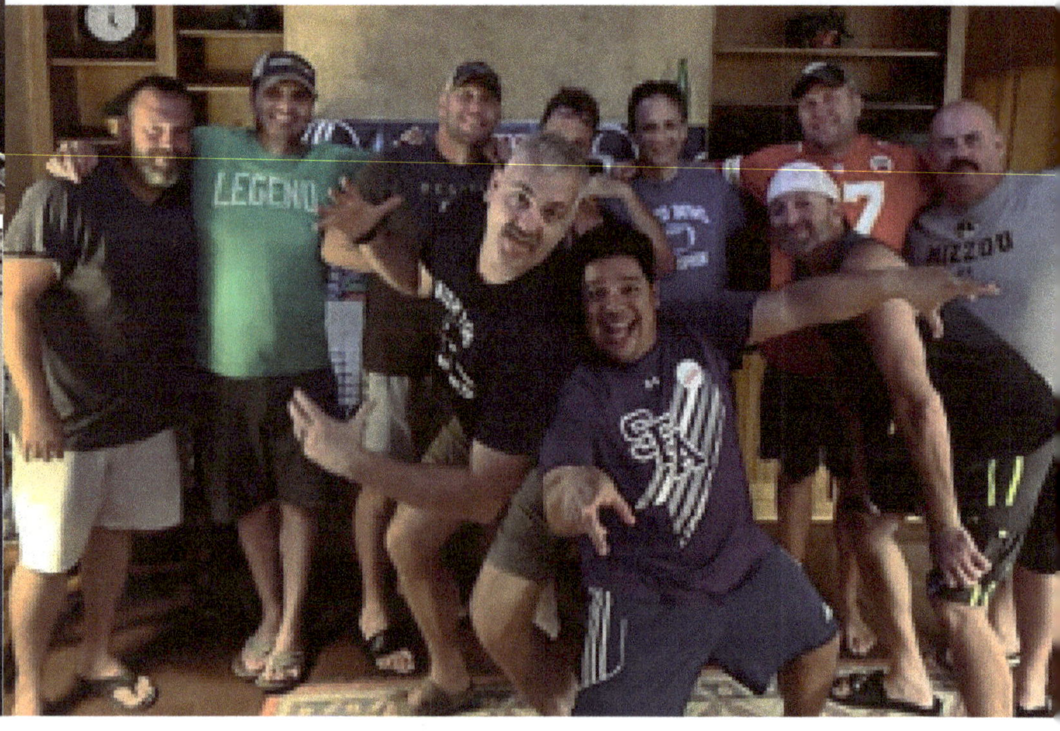
LEGEND
MIZZOU

Acknowledgements

My inspiration for writing this book is three-fold.

First, I was inspired by my friend, Mark Brandenburg (who is mentioned in the book), and my father in-law, Rolando Rodriguez. They had both published their first books earlier this year. Mark's book, *Fence Jumper*, is a suspense novel about political intrigue. In Roland's book, *El Columpio* (English translation is *The Porch Swing*), he recounts his stories growing up in Del Rio while sharing family history with his loved ones.

Second, both of my children are gifted writers. My daughter, Maya, is an avid reader, gifted writer, and future teacher. I believe she has a passion to write books of her own one day. My son is a typical 16-year-old boy obsessed with sports. He reads only what is mandated and doesn't write unless it's for a grade. Despite that, he has always scored extremely well on his writing and does have a gift that I wasn't blessed with. I want them to know that you can always stretch yourself and try new things even if you are a "boomer," as they call me.

Lastly, my wife, Addie, is an inspiration for just about everything I do. She loves the Lord, loves our kids, and has helped me build a better life than I ever could have hoped for. Thanks for your love and support. I definitely outkicked my coverage with her.

Although this book is simply meant to be a series of fun short stories, there is also a slight commentary on our current culture. By no means do I condone some of the actions you will read about, but I do think we have passed the point of letting the maturing process naturally happen. When I was in grade school in Minnesota, Tom, Dan, and I would ride our bikes to the next county with no GPS to guide us. Now, many kids aren't allowed to play in their own front yard without supervision.

I don't know what the right balance is between the freedom we had growing up and the security we now provide our kids, but my guess is we passed the Goldilocks porridge point somewhere along the way.

About the Author!

I live in Keller, TX with my amazing wife, Addie, and a couple of awesome teenagers. My daughter, Maya, is a freshman at Dallas Baptist University. My son, Josh, plays football at Byron Nelson High School. I've had a blast watching them grow up and look forward to witnessing the next phase of their journey. I've been fortunate enough to work for a world-class company I am proud to be at for 25 years, and I'm surrounded by talented people every day.

[The family in Long Beach, CA in 2022]

Follow my social media platforms.

Facebook: Michael Engstrom
Instagram: michael.engstrom1

www.ingramcontent.com/pod-product-compliance
Lightning Source LLC
Chambersburg PA
CBHW051212120626
46547CB00013B/1315